ISBN 978-1-334-40241-8
PIBN 10671199

1 MONTH OF
FREE
READING

at
www.ForgottenBooks.com

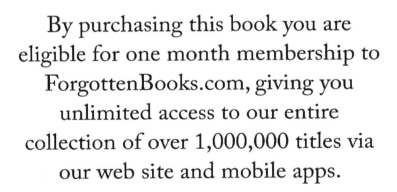

By purchasing this book you are eligible for one month membership to ForgottenBooks.com, giving you unlimited access to our entire collection of over 1,000,000 titles via our web site and mobile apps.

To claim your free month visit:
www.forgottenbooks.com/free671199

English
Français
Deutsche
Italiano
Español
Português

www.forgottenbooks.com

Mythology Photography **Fiction**
Fishing Christianity **Art** Cooking
Essays Buddhism Freemasonry
Medicine **Biology** Music **Ancient
Egypt** Evolution Carpentry Physics
Dance Geology **Mathematics** Fitness
Shakespeare **Folklore** Yoga Marketing
Confidence Immortality Biographies
Poetry **Psychology** Witchcraft
Electronics Chemistry History **Law**
Accounting **Philosophy** Anthropology
Alchemy Drama Quantum Mechanics
Atheism Sexual Health **Ancient History**
Entrepreneurship Languages Sport
Paleontology Needlework Islam
Metaphysics Investment Archaeology
Parenting Statistics Criminology
Motivational

THE
LIBERTINE:

Wing # S 2857

W.O. 67829

A
TRAGEDY.

Acted by His

ROYAL HIGHNESS's Servants.

Written by

THO. SHADWELL.

LONDON,

Printed by T. N. for *Henry Herringman*, at the *Anchor*,
in the Lower Walk of the *New Exchange*. 1676.

VIRTUTE ET FIDE.

Robert Harley of Bramton Castle in the County of Hereford Esq.

To the most Illustrious Prince

WILLIAM,

Duke, Marquis, and Earl

O F

NEWCASTLE, &c.

May it please your Grace,

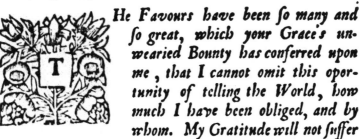

THe *Favours have been so many and so great, which your Grace's un-wearied Bounty has conferred upon me, that I cannot omit this oportunity of telling the World, how much I have been obliged, and by whom. My Gratitude will not suffer me to smother the favours in silence; nor the Pride they have rais'd me to, let me conceal the Name of so Excellent a Patron. The honour of being favoured by the great Newcastle, is equal with any real Merit, I am sure infinitely above mine. Yet the encouragement I receive from your Grace, is the certain way to make*

A 2   *the*

The Epistle Dedicatory.

the World believe I have some desert, or to create in me the most favourable thoughts of my self. My Name may thus, when otherwise it would perish, live in after Ages, under the protection of your Grace's, which, is famous abroad, and will be Eterniz'd in this Nation, for your Wit beyond all Poets; Judgment and Prudence, before all Statesmen; Courage and Conduct, above all Generals; Constancy and Loyalty, beyond all Subjects; Vertue and Temperance, above all Philosophers; for skill in Weapons, and Horsemanship, and all other Arts befitting your Quality, excelling all Noblemen: And lastly, for those eminent Services in defence of your King and Countrey, with an Interest and Power much exceeding all, and with Loyalty equalling any Nobleman. And indeed, the first was so great, that it might justly have made the greatest Prince afraid of it, had it not been so strongly secured by the latter.

All these Heroick Qualities I admired, and worshipped at a distance, before I had the Honour to wait upon your Grace at your House. For so vast was your Bounty to me, as to find me out in my obscurity, and oblige me several years, before you saw me at Welbeck; where (when I arrived) I found a Respect so extremely above the meanness of my Condition, that I still received it with blushes; having had nothing to recommend me, (but the Birth and Education, without the Fortune of a Gentleman) besides some Writings of mine, which your Grace was pleased to like. Then was soon added to my former Worship and Admiration,

miration, infinite Love, and infinite Gratitude, and a
Pride of being favour'd by one, in whom I observ'd a Ma-
jefly equal with greateft Princes, yet Affability exceeding
ordinary Gentlemen. A Greatnefs, that none e'r ap-
proached without Awe, or parted from without Satisfa-
Etion.

Then (by the great honour I had to be daily admitted
into your Grace's publick and private Converfation)
I obferved that admirable Experience and Judgment
furmounting all the Old, and that vigoroufnefs of Wit, and
fmartnefs of Expreffion, exceeding all the Young, I ever
knew; and not onely in fharp and apt Replies, the moft
excellent way of purfuing a Difcourfe; but (which is
much more difficult) by giving eafie and unforced occa-
fions, the moft admirable way of begining one; and all
this adapted to men of all Circumstances and Conditions.
Your Grace being able to difcourfe with every man in his
own way, which, as it fhows you to be a moft accurate Ob-
ferver of all mens tempers, fo it fhows your Excellency in
all their Arts. But when I had the favour daily to be
admitted to your Grace's more retired Converfation, when
I alone enjoyed the honour, I muft declare, I never fpent
my hours with that pleafure, or improvement; nor fhall
I ever enough acknowledge that, and the reft of the Ho-
nours done me by your Grace, as much above my Condition
as my Merit.

And

The Epiſtle Dedicatory.

And now, my Lord, after all this, imagine not I intend this ſmall Preſent of a Play (though favoured here by thoſe I moſt wiſh it ſhould be) as any return ; for all the Services of my life cannot make a ſufficient one. I onely lay hold on this occaſion, to publiſh to the World your great Favours, and the grateful Acknowledgments of,

My moſt Noble Lord,

Your Grace's

Moſt obliged, humble,

and obedient Servant,

THO. SHADWELL.

PREFACE.

He ſtory from which I took the hint of this Play, is famous all over *Spain*, *Italy*, and *France*: It was firſt put into a *Spaniſh* Play (as I have been told) the *Spaniards* having a Tradition (which they believe) of ſuch a vicious *Spaniard*, as is repreſented in this Play. From them the *Italian* Comedians took it, and from them the *French* took it, and four ſeveral *French* Plays were made upon the Story.

The Character of the *Libertine*, and conſequently thoſe of his Friends, are borrow'd; but all the Plot, till the latter end of the Fourth Act, is new: And all the reſt is very much varied from any thing which has been done upon the Subject.

I hope the Readers will excuſe the Irregularities of the Play, when they conſider, that the Extravagance of the Subject forced me to it: And I had rather try new ways to pleaſe, than to write on in the ſame Road, as too many do. I hope that the ſevereſt Reader will not be offended at the repreſentation of thoſe Vices, on

which

The Epiſtle Dedicatory.

And now, my Lord, after all this, imagine not I intend this ſmall Preſent of a Play (though favoured here by thoſe I moſt wiſh it ſhould be) as any return; for all the Services of my life cannot make a ſufficient one.   I onely lay hold on this occaſion, to publiſh to the World your great Favours, and the grateful Acknowledgments of,

My moſt Noble Lord,

Your Grace's

Moſt obliged, humble,

and obedient Servant,

· THO. SHADWELL.

Conqueſt of China. But he ought not to be called a Poet, who cannot write ten times a better in three weeks.

I cannot here paſs by his ſawcy Epiſtle to this *Conqueſt,* which (inſtead of expreſſions of juſt reſpect, due to the Birth and Merit of his Patron) is ſtuffed with railing againſt others. And firſt, he begins with the vanity of his Tribe. What Tribe that really is, it is not hard to gheſs; but all the Poets will bear me witneſs it is not theirs, who are ſufficiently ſatisfied, that he is no more a Poet than Servant to his Majeſty, as he preſumes to write himſelf; which I wonder he will do, ſince Protections are taken off: I know not what Place he is Sworn into in Extraordinary, but I am ſure there is no ſuch thing as Poet in Extraordinary.

But I wonder (after all his railing) he will call theſe Poets his Brethren; if they were, me-thinks he might have more natural affection than to abuſe his Brethren: but he might have ſpared that Title, for we can find no manner of Relation betwixt him and them; for they are all Gentlemen, that will not own him, or keep him company: and that, perhaps, is the cauſe which makes him ſo angry with them, to tax them, in his ill-manner'd Epiſtle, with Impudence, which he (having a particular affection for his own vice) calls by the name of Frailty. Impudence indeed is a very pretty Frailty.

But (what ever the Poets are guilty of) I wiſh he had as much of Poetry in him, as he has of that Frailty, for the good of the Duke's Theatre; they might then

have

have hopes of gaining as much by his good Senfe, as as they have loft by his Fuftian.

Thus much I thought fit to fay in vindication of the Poets, though, I think, he has not Authority enough (with men of fenfe) to fix any calumny upon the Tribe, as he calls it. For which reafon I fhall never trouble my felf to take notice of him hereafter, fince all men of Wit will think, that he can do the Poets no greater injury, than pretending to be one.   Nor had I laid fo much in anfwer to his courfe railing, but to reprehend his Arrogance, and lead him to a little better knowledge of himfelf; nor does his bafe Language in his *Poftfcript* deferve a better Return.

P R O-

PROLOGUE.

OUr Author sent me hither for a Scout,
    To spy what bloudy Criticks were come out ;
Those Piccaroons in Wit, wh'infest this Road,
And snap both Friend and Foe that come abroad.
This savage Party crueller appears,
Than in the Channel Ostend Privateers.
You in this Road, or sink, or plunder all,
Remorsle's as a Storm on us you fall :
But as a Merchant, when by storms distress'd,
Flings out his bulkey Goods to save the rest,
Hoping a Calm may come, he keeps the best.
In this black Tempest which o'r us impends,
Near Rocks and Quicksands, and no Ports of Friends,
Our Poet gives this over to your rage,
The most irregular Play upon the Stage,
As wild and as extravagant as th'Age.
Now, angry men, to all your splenes give vent ;
When all your fury has on this been spent,
Else-where you with much worse shall be content.
The Poet has no hopes you'll be appeas'd,
Who come on purpose but to be displeas'd.
Such corrupt Judges should excepted be,
Who can condemn before they hear or see.
Ne'r were such bloudy Criticks yet in fashion ;
You damn by absolute Predestination.
But why so many to run one man down ?
It were a mighty triumph when y'have done.
Our scarcity of Plays you should not blame,
When by foul poaching, so destroy the Game.
Let him but have fair play, and he may then
Write himself into favour once again.
If after this your anger you'll reveal,
To Cæsar he must make his just appeal ;
There Mercy and Judgment equally do meet,
To pardon Faults, and to encourage Wit.

The

The Persons represented.

Don John.	THe Libertine ; a rash fearless Man, guilty of all Vice.
Don Antonio. Don Lopez. }	His two Friends.
Don Octavio.	Brother to Maria.
Jacomo.	Don John's Man.
Leonora.	Don John's Mistris, abused by him, yet follows him for Love.
Maria,	Her Maid, abused by Don John, and following him for Revenge.
Don Francisco.	Father to Clara and Flavia.
Clara. Flavia. }	His Daughters.
Six Women.	All Wives to Don John.
Hermit.	
Two Gentlemen.	Intended for Husbands to Clara and Flavia.
Ghosts.	
Shepherds and Shepherdesses.	
Old Woman.	
Officer and Souldiers.	
Singers, Servants, Attendants.	

THE

THE
LIBERTINE.

ACT I.

Enter Don John, Don Lopez, Don Antonio, Jacomo,
Don John's *Valet.*

D. Joh. THus far without a bound we have enjoy'd
  Our prosp'rous pleasures, which dull Fools call
            [Sins ;
Laugh'd at old feeble Judges, and weak Laws ;
And at the fond fantastick thing, call'd Conscience,
Which serves for nothing but to make men Cowards ;
An idle fear of future misery ;
And is yet worse than all that we can fear.
 D. Lop. Conscience made up of dark and horrid thoughts,
Rais'd from the fumes of a distemper'd Spleen.
 D. Anto. A senfless fear, would make us contradict
The onely certain Guide, Infallible Nature ;
And at the call of Melancholly Fools,
(Who stile all actions which they like not, Sins)
To silence all our Natural appetites.
 D. John. Yet those conscientious Fools, that would persuade us
To I know not what, which they call Piety,
Have in reserve private delicious sins,
Great as the happy Libertine enjoys,
With which, in corners, wantonly they roul.
 D. Lop. Don *John,* thou art our Oracle ; thou hast
Dispell'd the fumes which once clowded our brains.
       B   *D. Anto.*

D. Ant. By thee, we have got loose from Education,
And the dull slavery of Pupillage,
Recover'd all the liberty of Nature,
Our own strong Reason now can go alone,
Without the feeble props of splenatick Fools,
Who contradict our common Mother, Nature.

D. Joh. Nature gave us our Senses, which we please :
Nor does our Reason War against our Sense.
By Nature's order Sense should guide our Reason,
Since to the mind all objects Sense conveys.
But Fools for shaddows lose substantial pleasures,
For idle tales abandon true delight,
And solid joys of day, for empty dreams at night.
Away, thou foolish thing, thou chollick of the mind,
Thou Worm by ill-digesting stomachs bred :
In spight of thee, we'll surfeit in delights,
And never think ought can be ill that's pleasant.

Jacom. A most excellent Sermon, and no doubt, Gentlemen,
you have edifi'd much by it.

D. Joh. Away ! thou formal phlegmatick Coxcomb, thou
Hast neither courage nor yet wit enough
To sin thus. Thou art my dull conscientious Pimp.
And when I am wanton with my Whore within,
Thou, with thy Beads and Pray'r-book, keep'st the door.

Jacom. Sir, I find your Worship is no more afraid to be damn'd,
than other fashionable Gentlemen of the Age : but, me-thinks,
Halters and Axes should terrifie you. With reverence to your
Worships, I've seen civiller men hang'd, and men of as pretty
parts too. There's scarce a City in *Spain* but is too hot for you,
you have committed such outrages wheresoe'r you come.

D. Lop. Come, for diversion, pray let's hear your Fool preach
a little.

Jaco. For my part, I cannot but be troubled, that I shall lose
my honour by you, Sir; for people will be apt to say, *Like Master, like Man.*

D. Joh. Your honour, Rascal, a Sow-gelder may better pretend to it.

Jacom. But I have another scruple, Sir.

D. Joh.

D. Joh. What's that?

Jacom. I fear I shall be hang'd in your company.

D. Joh. That's an honour you will ne'r have courage to deserve.

Jacom It is an honour I am not ambitious of.

D. Lop. Why does the Fool talk of hanging? we scorn all Laws.

Jacom. It seems so, or you would not have cut your Elder Brother's throat. *Don Lopez.*

D. Lop. Why, you Coxcomb, he kept a good Estate from me, and I could not Whore and Revel sufficiently without it.

D. Anto. Look you, *Jacomo*, had he not reason?

Jacom. Yes, *Antonio*, so had you to get both your Sisters with Child; 'twas very civil, I take it.

D. Anto. Yes, you Fool, they were lusty young handsome Wenches, and pleas'd my appetite. Besides, I sav'd the Honour of the Family by it; for if I had not, some body else would.

Jacom. O horrid villany!
But you are both Saints to my hopeful Master;
I'll turn him loose to *Belzebub* himself,
He shall out-do him at his own Weapons.

D. Joh. I, you Rascal.

Jacom. Oh no, Sir, you are as innocent. To cause your good old Father to be kill'd was nothing.

D. Joh. It was something, and a good thing too, Sirra: his whole design was to debar me of my pleasures: he kept his purse from me, and could not be content with that, but still would preach his senseless Morals to me, his old dull foolish stuff against my pleasure. I caus'd him to be sent I know not whether. But he believ'd he was to go to Heav'n; I care not where he is, since I am rid of him.

Jacom. Cutting his throat was a very good return for his begetting of you.

D. Joh. That was before he was aware on't, 'twas for his own sake, he ne'r thought of me in the business.

Jacom. Heav'n bless us!

D. Joh. You Dog, I shall beat out your brains, if you dare be so impudent as to pray in my company.

Jacom.

Jacom. Good Sir, I have done, I have done——

D. Lop. Prethee let the infipid Fool go on.

D. Ant. Let's hear the Coxcomb number up your crimes,
The patterns we intend to imitate.

Jacom. Sir, let me lay your horrid crimes before you:
The unhappy minute may perhaps arrive,
When the fenfe of 'em may make you penitent.

D. Anto. 'Twere better thou wer't hang'd.

D. Lop. Repent! Cowards and Fools do that.

D. Joh. Your valiant well-bred Gentlemen never repent:
But what fhould I repent of?

Jacom. After the murder of your Father, the brave *Don Pe-dro*, Governour of *Sevil*, for whom the Town are ftill in grief,
was, in his own houfe, barb'roufly kill d by you.

D. Joh. Barbaroufly, you lie, you Rafcal, 'twas finely done;
I run him through the Lungs as handfomely, and kill'd him as
decently, and as like a Gentleman as could be. The jealous
Coxcomb deferv'd death, he kept his Sifter from me; her eyes
would have kill'd me if I had not enjoy'd her, which I could
not do without killing him: Befides, I was alone, and kill'd him
hand to fift.

Jacom. I never knew you go to Church but to take Sanctuary
for a Murder, or to rob Churches of their Plate.

D. Joh. Heav'n needs not be ferv'd in Plate, but I had ufe
on't.

Jacom. How often have you fcal'd the Walls of Monafteries?
Two Nuns, I know, you ravifh'd, and a third you dangeroufly
wounded for her violent refiftance.

D. Joh. The perverfe Jades were uncivill, and deferv'd fuch
ufage.

Jacom. Some thirty Murders, Rapes innumerable, frequent
Sacrilege, Parricide; in fhort, not one in all the Catalogue of
Sins have fcap'd you.

D. Joh. My bufinefs is my pleafure, that end I will always
compafs, without fcrupling the means; there is no right or
wrong, but what conduces to, or hinders pleafure. But, you tedious infipid Rafcal, if I hear more of your Morality, I will Car-
bonado you.

D. Ant.

D. Anto. We live the life of Sense, which no fantastick thing, call'd Reason, shall controul.

D. Lop. My reason tells me, I must please my Sense.

D. Job. My appetites are all I'm sure I have from Heav'n, since they are Natural, and them I always will obey.

Jacom. I doubt it not, Sir, therefore I desire to shake hands and part.

D. Job. D' ye hear, Dog, talk once more of parting, and I will saw your Wind-pipe. I could find in my heart to cut your Rascal's Nose off, and save the Pox a labour : I'll do't, Sirra, have at you.

Jacom. Good Sir, be not so transported ; I will live, Sir, and will serve you in any thing ; I'll fetch a Wench, or any thing in the world Sir. O how I tremble at this Tyrant's rage.   [*aside.*

D. Anto. Come, 'tis night, we lose time to our adventures.

D. Lop. I have bespoke Musick for our Serenading.

D. Job. Let's on, and live the noble life of Sense.
To all the powers of Love and mighty Lust,
In spight of formal Fops I will be just.
What ways soe'r conduce to my delight,
My Sense instructs me, I must think 'em right.
On, on, my Soul, and make no stop in pleasure,
They're dull insipid Fools that live by measure.

                    [*Exeunt all but Jacomo.*

Jacom. What will become of me? if I should leave him, he's so revengeful, he would travel o'r all *Spain* to find me out, and cut my throat. I cannot live long with him neither : I shall be hang'd, or knock'd o'th' head, or share some dreadful Fate or other with him. 'Tis just between him and me, as between the Devil and the Witch, Who repents her bargain, and would be free from future ills, but for the fear of present durst not venture.

                    Enter Leonora.

Here comes *Leonora,* one of those multitudes of Ladies, he has sworn, li'd to, and betray'd.

Leon. Jacomo, where is *Don John?* I could not live to endure
                              a longer

a longer absence from him. I have sigh'd and wept my self away: I move, but have no life left in me. His coldness and his absence have given me fearful and killing apprehensions. Where is my Dear?

Jacom. Your Dear, Madam! he's your's no more.

Leon. Heav'n! what do I hear? Speak, is he dead?

Jacom. To you he is.

Leon. Ah me, has he forgot his Vows and Oaths? Has he no Conscience, Faith, or Honour left?

Jacom. Left, Madam, he ne'r had any.

Leon. It is impossible, you speak this out of malice sure.

Jacom. There's no man knows him better than I do. I have a greater respect for you, than for any he has betray'd, and will undeceive you : he is the most perfidious Wretch alive.

Leon. Has he forgot the Sacred Contract, which was made privately betwixt us, and confirm'd before the altar, during the time of holy Mass?

Jacom. All times and places are alike to him.

Leon. Oh how assiduous was he in his passion! how many thousand vows and sighs he breath'd! what tears he wept, seeming to suffer all the cruel pangs which Lovers e'r endur'd! how eloquent were all his words and actions!

Jacom. His person and his parts are excellent, but his base vices are beyond all measure : why would you believe him?

Leon. My own love brib'd me to believe him : I saw the man I lov'd more than the world. Oft on his knees, with his eyes up to Heav'n, kissing my hand with such an amorous heat, and with such ardor, breathing fervent vows of loyal Love, and venting sad complaints of extreme sufferings. I poor easie Soul, flattering my self to think he meant as I did, lost all my Sexes faculty, Dissembling; and in a moneth must I be thus betray'd?

Jacom. Poor Lady! I cannot but have bowels for you; your sad Narration makes me weep in sadness: but you are better us'd than others. I ne'r knew him constant a fortnight before.

Leon. Then, then he promis'd he would marry me.

Jacom. If he were to live here one moneth longer, he wou'd marry half the Town, ugly and handsome, old and young;

nothing

nothing that's Female comes amiſs to him ———

Leon. Does he not fear a thunderbolt from Heav'n.

Jacom. No, nor a Devil from Hell. He owns no Deity but his voluptuous appetite, whoſe ſatisfaction he will compaſs by Murders, Rapes, Treaſons, or ought elſe. But pray let me ask you one civil queſtion, Did you not give him earneſt of your Body, Madam.

Leon. Mock not my miſery.
Oh! that confounds me. Ah! I thought him true, and lov'd him ſo, I could deny him nothing.

Jacom. Why, there 'tis; I fear you have, or elſe he wou'd have marri'd you: he has marri'd ſix within this moneth, and promis'd fifteen more, all whom he has enjoy'd, and left, and is this night gone on ſome new adventure, ſome Rape or Murder, ſome ſuch petty thing.

Leon. Oh Monſter of impiety!
Oh falſe *Don John*! wonder of cruelty!   [*She ſwounds.*

Jacom. What a pox does ſhe ſwound at the news! Alas! poor Soul, ſhe has mov'd me now to pity, as ſhe did to love. Ha! the place is private——— If I ſhould make uſe of a Natural Receit to refreſh her, and bring her to life again, 'twould be a great pleaſure to me, and no trouble to her. Hum! 'tis very private, and I dare ſin in private. A deuce take her, ſhe revives, and pre-vents me.

Leon. Where is the cruel Tyrant! inhumane Monſter! but I will ſtrive to fortifie my ſelf. But Oh my misfortune! Oh my miſery! Under what ſtrange Enchantments am I bound? Could he be yet a thouſand times more impious, I could not chuſe but love his perſon ſtill.

Jacom. Be not ſo paſſionate; if you could be diſcreet, and love your ſelf, I'd put you in a way to eaſe your grief now, and all your cares hereafter.

Leon. If you can now eaſe an afflicted Woman, who elſe muſt ſhortly rid her ſelf of life, imploy your charity; 'twas never plac'd yet on a Wretch needed it more than I.

Jacom. If Loyalty in a Lover be a Jewel! ſay no more, I can tell you where you may have it—

Leon. Speak not of truth in man, it is impoſſible.

                                                              Jaco it.

Jacom. Pardon me, I speak on my own knowledge.

Leon. Is your Master true then? and have you happily deceiv'd me? Speak.

Jacom. As true as all the power of Hell can make him.

Leon. If he be false, let all the world be so.

Jacom. There's another-guess man than he, Madam.

Leon. Another! who can that be?

No, no, there's no truth found in the Sex.   [*Aside.*

Jacom. He is a civil vertuous and discreet sober person.

Leon. Can there be such a man? what does he mean?

Jacom. There is, Madam, a man of goodly presence too——
Something inclining to be fat, of a round plump face, with
quick and sparkling eyes, and mouth of cheerful overture——
His nose, which is the onely fault, is somewhat short, but that's
no matter; his hair and eye-brows black, and so forth.

Leon. How! he may perhaps be brib'd by some other man,
and what he said of his Master may be false.

Jacom. How she surveys me! Fa-la-la
                              [*Sings, and struts about.*

Leon. Who is this you speak of?

Jacom. A man, who, envy must confess, has excellent parts,
but those are gifts, gifts—— meer gifts —— thanks be to
Heav'n for them.

Leon. But shall I never know his name?

Jacom. He's one, whom many Ladies have honour'd with
their affection; but no more of that. They have met disdain,
and so forth. But he'll be content to marry you. Fa-la-la-la
                                            [*Sings.*

Leon. Again I ask you who he is?

Jacom. Lord, how inapprehensive she is? Can you not guess?

Leon. No.

Jacom. Your humble Servant, Madam.

Leon. Yours, Sir.

Jacom. It is my self in person; and upon my honour, I will be
true and constant to you.

Leon. Insolent Varlet! am I faln so low to be thy scorn?

Jacom. Scorn! as I am a Christian Soul, I am in earnest.

Leon. Audacious Villain! Impudence it self!

Jacom.

Jacom. Ah, Madam ! your Servant, your true Lover muſt endure a thouſand ſuch bobs from his Miſtris ; I can bear, Madam, I can.

Leon. Becauſe thy Maſter has betray'd me, am I become ſo infamous ?

Jacom. 'Tis ſomething hard, Madam, to preſerve a good reputation in his company ; I can ſcarce do't my ſelf.

Leon. Am I ſo miſerable to deſcend to his man ?

Jacom. Deſcend, ſay you : Ha, ha, ha !

Leon. Now I perceive all's falſe which you have ſaid of him. Farewell, you baſe ingrateful Fellow.

Jacom. Hold, Madam, come in the morning and I will place you in the next room, where you ſhall over-hear our diſcourſe. You'll ſoon diſcover the miſtake, and find who 'tis that loves you. Retire, Madam, I hear ſome body coming.

[*Exeunt* Jacomo, Leonora.

Enter Don John *in the Street.*

D. Joh. Let me ſee, here lives a Lady: I have ſeen *Don Octavio* haunting about this houſe, and making private ſigns to her. I never ſaw her face, but am reſolv'd to enjoy her, becauſe he likes her ; beſides, ſhe's another Woman.

Enter Antonio.

Antonio, welcome to our place of randezvous. Well, what game! what adventure!

Enter Lopez.

Come, dear *Lopez.*

Anto. I have had a rare adventure.

Lop. What, dear *Antonio ?*

Ant. I ſaw at a *Vill* not far off, a grave mighty bearded Fool, drinking *Lemonado* with his Miſtris; I miſlik'd his face, pluck'd him by the Whiskers, pull'd all one ſide of his Beard off, fought with him, run him through the thigh, carri'd away his Miſtris,

C   ſerv'd serv'd her in her kind, and then let her go.

D. Joh. Gallantly perform'd, like a brave Souldier in an Enemies Countrey : When they will not pay Contribution, you fight for Forrage.

D. Lop. Pox on't, I have been damnably unfortunate ; I have neither beat man, nor lain with Woman to night, but faln in love most furiously : I dogg'd my new Mistris to her Lodging ; she's *Don Bernardo's* Sister, and shall be my Punk.

D. Joh. I could meet with no willing Dame, but was fain to commit a Rape to pass away the time.

D. Anto. Oh ! a Rape is the joy of my heart ; I love a Rape, upon my *Clavis*, exceedingly.

D. Joh. But mine, my Lads, was such a Rape, it ought to be Registred ; a noble and heroick Rape.

D. Lop. Ah ! dear *Don John* !

D. Anto. How was it ?

D. Joh. 'Twas in a Church, Boys.

D. Anto. Ah ! Gallant Leader !

D. Lop. Renown'd *Don John* !

D. Anto. Come, let's retire, you have done enough for once.

D. Joh. Not yet, *Antonio*, I have an Intrigue here.

Enter Fidlers.

Here are my Fidlers. Rank your selves close under this Window, and sing the Song I prepar'd.

SONG.

THou joy of all hearts, and delight of all eyes,
  Nature's chief Treasure, and Beauty's chief Prize,
    Look down, you'l discover,
  Here's a faithful young vigorous Lover ;
    With a heart full as true,
    As e'r languish'd for you ;
  Here's a faithful young vigorous Lover.

The Heart that was once a Monarch in's breast,
Is now your poor Captive, and can have no rest ;
'Twill never give over,
But about your sweet bosom will hover.
Dear Miss, let it in,
By Heav'n 'tis no sin ;
Here's a faithful young vigorous vigorous Lover.

D. Joh. Now Fidlers, be gone.

[*Window opens,* Maria *looks out, and flings a Paper down.*
Mar. Retire, my Dear *Octavia ;* read that Note. Adieu.
[*Exit* Mar.

D. Joh. Good, she takes me for *Octavio.* I warrant you, Boys,
I shall succeed in this adventure. Now my false Light assist me.
[*Reads by a dark Lantern.*

Reads. { *Go from this Window, within eight minutes you shall*
be admitted to the Garden dore. You know the
Sign.

Ha! the Sign, Gad she lies, I know not the Sign.

D. Anto. What will you do? you know not the Sign. Let's
away, and be contented this night.

D. Joh. My friends, if you love me, retire. I'll venture, though
Thunderbolts should fall upon my head.

D. Lop. Are you mad? as soon as she discovers the deceit,
she'll raise the house upon you, and you'll be murder'd.

D. Joh. She'll not raise the house for her own sake, but rather
grant me all I ask to keep her counsell.

D. Anto. 'Tis very dangerous: be careful of your self.

D. Joh. The more danger, the more delight: I hate the com-
mon road of pleasure. What! can I fear at such a time as this!
The cowardly Deer are valiant in their Rutting time. I say,
Be gone ———

D. Anto. We'll not dispute your commands. Good luck to
you.   [*Exeunt* Antonio, Lopez.

D. Joh. How shall I know this devillish Sign?

C 2   *Enter*

Enter Octavio *with Fidlers, and stands under*
Maria's *window.*

Ha! whom have we hear? some Serenading **Coxcomb.** Now
shall we have some damn'd Song or other, a *Cloris,* or a *Phillis*
at least.

SONG.

Cloris. When you disperse your influence,
　　Your dazling Beams are quick and clear,
　　You so surprize and wound the sense,
　　So bright a Miracle y'appear.
Admiring Mortals you astonish so,
　　No other Deity they know,
But think that all Divinity's below ————

　　One charming look from your illustrious Face,
　　Were able to subdue Mankind,
　　So sweet, so powerful a Grace
　　Makes all men Lovers but the blind:
Nor can they freedom by resistance gain,
　　For each embraces the soft Chain,
　　And never struggles with the pleasant pain.

Octa. Be gone! be gone! the Window opens.
D. Joh. 'Sdeath! this is *Octavio.* I must dispatch him, or he'll
spoil all; but I would fain hear the Sign first.
Mar. What strange mistake is this? Sure he did not receive
my Note, and then I am ruin'd.
Octa. She expects the Sign. Where's my Whistle? O here.
　　　　　　　　　　　　　　　　　　　[*Whistles*

D. Joh. I have found it, that must be the Sign————
Mar. I dare not speak aloud, go to the Garden door.
　　　　　　[*Don John rushes upon* Octavio, *and snatches*
　　　　　　　the Whistle out of his hand.
Octa. 'Sdeath, what Ruffian's this?
　　　　　　　　　　　　　　　　　　　　D. Joh.

D. Joh. One that will be sure to cut your throat.

Octa. Make not a promise to your self of what you cann't perform. [*Fight.*

D. Joh. I warrant you. Have at you.

Mar. O Heav'n! *Octavio's* fighting. Oh my heart!

Octa. Oh! I am slain——— [*Falls.*

D. Joh. I knew I should be as good as my word. I think you have it, Sir —— Ha! he's dying —— Now for the Lady—— I'll draw him further off, that his groans may not disturb our pleasure ——— Stay——— by your leave, Sir, I'll change Hat and Cloak with you, it may help me in my design.

Octav. O barbarous Villain! [*Dies.*

Mar. They have done fighting, and I hear no noise. Oh unfortunate Woman! my dear *Octavio's* kill'd———

Flora. Perhaps, Madam, he has kill'd the other. I'll down to the Garden door; if he be well, he'll come thither, as well to satisfie his appointment, as to take refuge. Your Brother's safe, he may come in securely ——— [*Ex. to the door.*

Mar. Haste! haste! Fly! fly! Oh *Octavio.* I'll follow her. [*She follows.*

D. Joh. Now for the Garden door. This Whistle will do me excellent service. Now good luck——— [*Goes to the door and whistles.*

Flo. Octavio?

D. Joh. The same.

Flo. Heav'n be prais'd, my Lady thought you had been kill'd.

D. Joh. I am unhurt: let's quickly to her.

Flo. Oh! he'll be over-joy'd to see you alive.

D. Joh. I'll make her more over-joy'd before I have done with her. This is a rare adventure!

Enter Maria *at the door.*

Flo. Here's your Jewel, Madam, speak softly.

Mar. O my dear *Octavio!* have I got you within these arms?

D. Joh. Ay, my Dear, unpierc'd by any thing but by your eyes.

Mar. Those will do you no hurt. But are you sure you are not wounded? *D. Joh.*

D. Joh. I am. Let me embrace my pretty Dear; and yet she may be a Blackamore for ought I know———

Mar. We'll retire to my Chamber. *Flora*, go out, and prepare us a Collation.

D. Jon. O admirable adventure! Come, my Delight.

[*Exeunt.*

Enter Don Lopez, Antonio, Jacomo.

Jac. Where's my pious Master?

D. Ant. We left him hereabouts. I wonder what he has done in his adventure: I believe he has had some busle.

D. Lop. I thought I heard fighting hereabout.

Jac. Gad forgive me! fighting! where! where!

D. Ant. O thou incorrigible Coward!

D. Lop. See, here's some of his handy-work; here's a man kill'd.

Jac. Another murder. Heav'n, what will become of me? I shall be hang'd, yet dare not run away from him.

Enter an Officer with a Guard, going the Round.

Officer. Stand! who are there?

D. Lop. We do stand, Rascal, we never use to run.

Jac. Now shall I be taken and hang'd for my Master's murder.

[*Offers to run.*

D. Ant. Stand, you Dog! offer once more to run, and I'll put Bilbow in your guts.

Jac. Gad forgive me! what will become of me?

Officer. What's here? a man murder'd? yield, you are my prisoners.

Jac. With all my heart! but as I hope to be sav'd, we did not kill him, Sir

Offic. These must be the murderers, disarm 'em.

D. Ant. How now, Rascal! disarm us!

D. Lop. We are not us'd to part with our Swords.

Jac. I care not a farthing for my Sword, 'tis at your service.

D. Ant. Do you hear, Rascal; keep it, and fight, or I'll swear the murder against you.

D. Lop.

D. Lop. Offer to flinch, and I'll run you through.

Offic. Take their Swords, or knock 'em down.

[*They fight.* Jacomo *offers to run,*
some of the Guards stop him.

Jac. A pox on't, I had as good fight and die, as be taken and be hang'd. [*Guards are beaten off.*

D. Lop. Are you gone, you Dogs? I have pinck'd some of you.

Jac. Ah Rogues! Villains! I have met with you.

D. Ant. O brave *Jacomo!* you fought like an imprison'd Rat: The Rogue had conceal'd Courage, and did not know it.

Jac. O Cowards! Rascals! a man can get no honour by fighting with such Poletroons! but for all that, I will prudently withdraw, this place will suddenly be too hot for us.

D. Lop. Once in your life you are in the right, *Jacomo.*

Jac. O good Sir, there is as much to be ascribed to Conduct, as to Courage, I assure you. [*Exeunt.*

Enter Don John *and* Maria *in her Chamber.*

Mar. Speak softly, my Dear; should my Brother hear us, we are ruin'd.

D. Joh. Though I can scarce contain my joy, I will. O she's a rare Creature in the dark, pray Heav'n she be so in the light.

Enter Flora *with a Candle; as soon as they discover*
Don John, *they shreike out.*

Mar. O Heav'n! I am ruin'd and betray'd.

Flo. He has *Octavio's* clothes on.

Mar. O he has murder'd him. My Brother shall revenge it.

D. Joh. I will cut his throat if he offers it.

Mar.
Flo. } Thieves! Murder! Murder! Thieves!

D. Joh. I will stop your shrill wind-pipes.

Enter

Enter Maria's Brother, with his Sword drawn.

Broth. 'Sdeath ! a man in my Sister's Chamber !
Have at you, Villain.
    D. Joh. Come on, Villain.   [Don John *kills the Brother.*
    Flo Murder ! Murder !
    Mar. O Villain, thou hast kill'd my Brother, and dishonour'd
me.

Enter five or six Servants, with drawn Swords.

O your Master's murder'd !
    D. Joh. So many of you ; 'tis no matter : your *Hero's* in
Plays beat five times as many. Have at you, Rogues.
          [*Maria runs away shrieking, and* Don John
           beats the Servants off, and stops Flora.
Now give me the Key of the Garden, or I'll murder thee.
    Flo. Murder ! Murder ! There, take it —— [*She runs away.*
    D. Joh. So, thus far it is well ; this was a brave adventure.
'Mongst all the Joys which in the world are sought,
None are so great as those by dangers bought.   [*Exit.*

ACT II.

Jacomo *solus.*

Jac. **W**Hat will this lead Master of mine do ? this Town of
Sevil will not much care for his company after his
last nights Atchievments : He must now either fly, or hang for't.
Ha ! me-thinks my bloud grows chill at the naming of that
dreadful word, *Hang* —— What will become of me ? I dare not
leave him, and yet I fear that I shall perish with him. He's certainly the first that ever set up a Religion to the Devil.

                                Enter

Enter Leonora.

Leon. I come to claim your promise; is *Don John* within ?

Jacom. No, Madam, but I expect him every minute. You see, Madam, what honour I have for you, for I venture my ears to do this.

Leon. You oblige me extremely; so great is the present pain of doubt, that we desire to lose it : though in exchange of certainty, that must afflict us more.

Jac. I hear him coming, withdraw quickly.

[*She withdraws.*

Enter Don John.

D. Joh. How now, Sir, what wise thoughts have you in your Noddle?

Jac. Why, Sir, I was considering how well I could endure to be hang'd.

D. Joh. And why so, Buffle?

Jac. Why you will force me to wait upon you in all your fortunes, and you are making what haste you can to the Gallows ———

D. Joh. Again at your reproofs. You insipid Rascal; I shall cut your ears off, Dog ———

Jac. Good Sir, I have done ; yet I cannot but admire, since you are resolv'd to go to the Devil, that you cannot be content with the common way of travelling, but must ride post to him.

D. Joh. Leave off your idle tales, found out by Priests to keep the Rabble in awe.

Jac. Oh horrid wickedness! If I may be bold to ask, what noble exploits did your Chivalry perform last night?

D. Joh. Why, Sir, I committed a Rape upon my Father's Monument.

Jac. Oh horror !

D. Joh. Do you start, you Villain ? Hah !

Jac. I, Sir, who I, Sir? not I, Sir.

D. Joh. D'hear, Rascal, let me not see a frown upon your

D   face

face ; if I do, I will cut your throat, you Rogue.

Jac. No, Sir, no, Sir, I warrant you ; I am in a very good humour, I assure you —— Heav'n deliver me !

D. Joh. Now listen and learn. I kill'd a Lady's Lover, and suppl'd his place, by stratagem enjoy'd her : In came her foolish Brother and surpriz'd me, but perish'd by my hand ; and I doubt not but I maul d three or four of his Servants.

[Jacomo *starts.*
[*Aside.*

Jac. Oh horrid fact !

D. Joh. Again, Villain, are you frowning ?

Jac. No, Sir, no, Sir ; don't think so ill of me, Sir. Heav'n send me from this wicked Wretch ! What will become of us, Sir ? we shall be apprehended.

D. Joh. Can you fear your Rascally Carcase, when I venture mine ? I observe always, those that have the most despicable persons, are most careful to preserve 'em.

Jac. Sir, I beg your pardon ; but I have an odd humour, makes me something unfit for your Worship's service.

D. Joh. What s that, Sirra ?

Jac. 'Tis a very odd one, I am almost asham'd to tell it to you.

D. Joh. Out with it, Fool ——

Jac. Why Sir, I cannot tell what is the reason, but I have a most unconquerable antipathy to Hemp. I could never endure a Bell-rope. Hanging is a kind of death I cannot abide, I am not able to endure it.

D. Joh. I have taken care to avoid that ; my friends are gone to hire a Vessel, and we'll to Sea together to seek a refuge, and a new Scene of pleasure.

Jac. All three, Sir ?

D. Joh. Yes, Sir. ——

Jac. Three as civil discreet sober persons, as a man wou'd wish to drink with.

Enter Leonora.

Leon. I can hold no longer !

D. Joh. 'Sdeath, you Dog, how came she here ?

Jac. I don't know, Sir, she stole in ——

Leon. What Witchcraft do I suffer under? that when I abhor his vices, I still love his person. Ah, *Don John!* have I deserv'd that you should fly me? are all your Oaths and Vows forgotten by you?

D. Joh. No, no; in these cases I always remember my Oaths, and never forget to break them.

Leon. Oh impiety!

Did I, for this, yield up my Honour to you? after you had sigh'd and languish'd many moneths, and shew'd all signs of a sincere affection, I trusted in your truth and constancy, without the Bond of Marriage, yielded up a Virgin's Treasure, all my Innocence, believ'd your solemn Contract, when you invok'd all the Pow'rs above to testifie your Vows.

D. Joh. They think much of us, why don't they witness 'em for you ———— Pish, 'tis nothing but a way of speaking, which young amorous Fellows have gotten ———

Leon. Did you not love me then? What injury had I e'r done you, that you shou'd feign affection to betray me?

D. Joh. Yes faith, I did love you, and shew'd you as frequent and as hearty signs of it as I could; and i'gad y'are an ungrateful Woman if you say the contrary.

Leon. O heav'n! Did you, and do not now? What crime have I committed, that could make you break your Vows and Oaths, and banish all your passion? Ah! with what tenderness have I receiv'd your feign'd affection, and ne'r thought I liv'd but in your presence; my love was too fervent to be counterfeit———

D. Joh. That I know not, for since your Sex are such dissemblers, they can hold out against, and seem to hate the men they love; why may they not seem to love the men they hate?

Leon. O cruel man! could I dissemble? had I a thousand lives, I ventur'd all each time I saw your face; nay, were I now discover'd, I should instantly be sacrific'd to my raging Brother's fury; and can I dissemble?

D. Joh. I do not know whether you do or no; you see I don't, I am something free with you.

Leon. And do you not love me then?

D. Joh. Faith, Madam, I lov'd you as long as I could for the

D 2 heart

heart and bloud of me, and there's an end of it; what a Devil would you have more?

Leon. O cruel man! how miserable have you made me!

D. Joh. Miserable! use variety as I do, and you'll not be miserable. Ah! there's nothing ~~so sweet to frail~~ humane flesh as variety.

Leon. Inhumane Creature! what have I been guilty of, that thou shouldst thus remove thy affections from me?

D. Joh. Guilty, no: but I have had enough of you, and I have done what I can for you, and there's no more to be said.

Leon. Tigers would have more pity than thou hast.

D. Joh. Unreasonable Woman! would you have a man love after enjoyment? I think the Devil's in you ——

Leon. Do you upbraid me with the rash effects of Love, which you caus'd in me? and do you hate me for what you ought to love me for? were you not many moneths with Vows and Oaths betraying me to that weakness? Ungrateful Monster!

D. Joh. Why the Devil did you not yield before? you Women always rook in Love; you'll never play upon the square with us.

Leon. False man! I yielded but too soon. Unfortunate Woman!

D. Joh. Your dissembling Arts and jilting tricks, taught you by your Mothers, and the phlegmatick coldness of your constitutions, make you so long in yielding; that we love out almost all our love before you begin, and yet you would have our love last as long as yours. I got the start of you a long way, and have reason to reach the Goal before you.

Leon. Did you not swear you wou'd for ever love me?

D. Joh. Why there 'tis; why did you put me to the trouble to swear it? If you Women would be honest, and follow the Dictates of Sense and Nature, we shou'd agree about the business presently, and never be forsworn for the matter.

Leon. Are Oaths so slighted by you? perfidious man!

D. Joh. Oaths! Snares to catch conceited Women with; I wou'd have sworn all the Oathes under the Sun; why I wou'd have committed Treason for you, and yet I knew I should be weary of you ——

Leon

Leon. I thought such love as mine might have deserv'd your constancy, false and ungrateful man!

D. Joh. Thus your own vanity, not we betray you. Each wo-man thinks, though men are false to others, that she is so fine a person, none can be so to her. You should not take our words of course in earnest.

Leon. Thus Devils do in Hell, who cruelly upbraid whom they have tempted thither.

D. Joh. In short, my constitution will not let me love you longer: and what ever some Hypocrites pretend, all mankind obey their constitutions, and cannot do otherwise ——

Leon. Heav'n, sure, will punish this vile treachery.

D. Joh. Do you then leave it to Heav'n, and trouble your self no farther about it.

Leon. Ye Sacred Pow'rs, who take care of injur'd innocence, assist me.

Enter Jacomo.

Jac. Sir, Sir! stand upon your guard.

D. Joh. How now! what's the matter?

Jac. Here's a whole Batalion of couragious Women come to charge you.

Enter Six Women.

D. Joh. Keep 'em out, you Villain.

Jac. I cannot, they over-run me.

D. Joh. What an inundation of Strumpets is here?

Leon. O Heav'n! I can stay no longer to be a witness of his falshood —— [*Exit* Leonora.

1. *Wom.* My Dear, I desire a word in private with you.

D. Joh. 'Faith, my Dear, I am something busie, but I love thee dearly. [*Aside.* A pox on thee!

2. *Wom. Don John*, a word: 'tis time now we should declare our marriage; 'tis now above three weeks.

D. Joh. Ay, we will do it suddenly ——

3. *Wom.* Pre'thee, Honey, what bus'ness can these idle Women have
have

have? send them packing, that we may confer about our affairs.

4. Wom. Lord! how am I amaz'd at the confidence of some Women! who are these that will not let one converse with one's own Husband ? By your leave, Ladies.

Jac. Now it works! tease him, Ladies, worry him soundly ———

5. Wom. Nay, by your leave, good Madam ; if you go to that. [*Pulls* Don John *from the other.*

6. Wom. Ladies, by all your leaves ; sure none of you will have the confidence to pretend an interest in this Gentleman——

D. Joh. I shall be torn in pieces : *Jacomo,* stand by me.

1. Lad. Lord, Madam, what's your meaning ? none ought to claim a right to another Woman's Husband, let me tell you that.

2. Lad. You are in the right, Madam. Therefore prethee, Dear, let's withdraw, and leave them ; I do not like their company.

D. Joh. Ay, presently, my Dear. What an excellent thing is a Woman before enjoyment, and how insipid after it!

4. Wom. Come, prethee, put these Women out of doubt, and let them know our Marriage.

D. Joh. To morrow we'll declare and celebrate our Nuptials.

6. Wom. Ladies, the short and the long on't is, you are very uncivil to press upon this Gentleman. Come, Love, e'en tell 'em the truth of the story ———

4. Wom. Uncivil, Madam, pardon me; one cannot be so in speaking to one's own.

3. Wom. That's true; she little thinks who that is.

6. Wom. To their own! Ha, ha, ha, that's true——— Come, Honey, keep 'em no longer in ignorance.

4. Wom. Come, Ladies, I will undeceive you all; think no further of this Gentleman, I say, think no further of him———

1. Wom. What can this mean ?

D. Joh. Hold, for Heav'n's sake; you know not what you do.

4. Wom. Yes, yes, I do; it shall all out: I'll send 'em away with Fleas in their Ears. Poor silly Creatures!

D. Joh. Now will Civil Wars arise ———

4. Wom.

4. Wom. Trouble your felves no longer about *Don John*, he is . mine ———— he is mine, Ladies————

All. Yours! ————

D. Joh. Pox on't, I muft fet a good face upon the buf'nefs; I fee murder will out————

6 Wom. Yours! that's pleafant; he's mine————

5. Wom. I have been too long patient; he is my Husband.

1. Wom. Yours, how can that be? I am fure I am his Wife.

3. Wom. Are you not afham'd, Ladies, to claim my Husband?

2. Wom. Are you all mad? I am fure I am marri'd to him.

All. You!

D. Joh. Look you, Ladies, a Man's but a Man; here's my Body, tak't among you as far as 'twill go. The Devil can't pleafe you all————

Jac. Pray, Ladies, will you difpatch; for there are a matter of fifteen more that are ready to put in their claims, and muft be heard in their order————

D. Joh. How now, Rogue? this is your fault, Sirra.

Jac. My fault, Sir, no; the Ladies fhall fee I am no Traitor. Look you, Ladies————

D. Joh. Peace, Villain, or I will cut your throat. Well, Ladies, know then, I am marri'd to one in this company; and to morrow morning, if you will repair to this place, I will declare my Marriage, which now, for fome fecret Reafons, I am oblig'd to conceal —— Now will each Strumpet think 'tis her I mean.

1. Wom. That's well enough.

4. Wom. I knew he would own me at laft.

3. Wom. Now they will foon fee their errors.

5. Now we'll conceal it no longer, Deareft.

D. Joh. No, no, I warrant you ————

6. Wom. Lord how blank thefe Ladies will look.

2. Wom. Poor Ladies ———

Jac. Ladies, pray let me ask a queftion, which of you is really marri'd to him?

Omn. I, I, I

D. Joh. 'Sdeath, you Son of a Baboon. Come, Pox on't, why fhould I dally any longer! why fhould I conceal my good actions! in one word, I am married to every one of you, and have

above

above fourscore more; nor will I ever give over, till I have as many Wives and Concubines as the *Grand Seignior.*

Jac. A very modest civil person truly ——

4. *Wom.* O horrid Villain!

6. *Wom.* Perfidious Monster!

Enter Don Lopez *and* Antonio.

D. Ant. How now, *Don John*; Hah! you are a rav'nous Bird of prey indeed; do you fly at no less than a whole Covee of Whores at once? you scorn a single Strumpet for your Quarry.

Ant. What, in tears too! Fie, *Don John*; thou art the most ungentle Knight alive: use your Ladies civilly for shame.

D. Joh. Ay, before the Victory, I grant you; but after it, they should wear Chains, and follow the Conqueror's Chariot.

D. Lop. Alas, poor Harlots!

D. Joh. Peace, peace, good words; these are certain Animals call'd Wives, and all of 'em are my Wives: Do you call a man of Honour's Wives, Harlots? out, on't.

1. *Wom.* Perfidious Monster!

Ant. Excellent!

D. Joh. Come on, you are come very opportunely, to help to celebrate my several and respective Weddings. Come, my Dears; faith we will have a Ballad at our Weddings. Where are my Fidlers?

6. *Wom.* O salvage Beast!

4. *Wom.* Inhumane Villain! revenge shall follow.

D. Joh. Pox on revenge. Call in my Minstrils.

Enter Fidlers.

Come, sing my *Epithalamium.*

SONG.

SONG.

Since Liberty, Nature for all has design'd,
A pox on the Fool who to one is confin'd.
    All Creatures besides,
  When they please change their Brides.
All Females they get when they can,
Whilst they nothing but Nature obey,
   How happy, how happy are they?
But the silly fond Animal, Man,
Makes Laws 'gainst himself, which his Appetites sway;
    Poor Fools, how unhappy are they?
Chor. Since Liberty, Nature for all has design'd,
  A pox on the Fool who to one is confin'd.

At the first going down, a Woman is good,
But when e'er she comes up, I'll ne'r chew the Cud,
    But out she shall go,
    And I'll serve 'em all so.
When with one my stomach is cloy'd,
Another shall soon be enjoy'd.
   Then how happy, how happy are we?
Let the Coxcomb, when weary, drudge on,
And foolishly stay when he wou'd fain be gone.
    Poor Fool! how unhappy is he?
Chor. At the first going down, &c.

Let the Rabble obey, I'll live like a Man,
Who, by Nature, is free to enjoy all he can:
    Wise Nature does teach
   More truth than Fools preach;
They bind us, but she gives us ease.
I'll revel and love where I please.
She, she's my infallible Guide.
  But were the bless'd freedom deni'd
Of variety in the things we love best,
    Dull Man were the slavishest Beast.
Chor. Let the Rabble obey, &c.

E   D. Joh.

D. Joh. Come, how do you like this? let's be merry, my Brides.

4. Wom. O monstrous Traitor! do you mock our misery?

D. Joh. Good Spouse, be not passionate—— faith we'll have a Dance. Strike up——   [*Dance.*

D. Lop. Be comforted, good Ladies; you have Companions in your misfortunes ——

D. Ant. He has been marri'd in all the Cities of *Spain* ; what a breed of *Don Johns* shall we have?

D. Joh. Come, Sweethearts; you must be civil to these Gentlemen ; they are my Friends, and men of Honour.

6. Wom. Men of Honour! they are Devils if they be your Friends.

D. Joh. I hate unreasonable, unconscionable fellows, who when they are weary of their Wives, will still keep 'em from other men. Gentlemen, ye shall command mine.

4. Wom. Thinkest thou I will out-live this affront?

D. Joh. I'll trust you for that, there's ne'r a *Lucrece* now adays, the Sex has learnt more wit since. Let me see, *Antonio*, thou shalt have for thy present use, let me see, my sixth Wife —— 'faith she's a pretty buxom Wench, and deserves hearty usage from thee.

6. Wom. Traitor! I'll be reveng'd on all thy treachery.

Ant. A mettel'd Girl, I like her well : she'll endure a Rape gallantly. I love resistance, it endears the pleasure.

D. Joh. And, *Lopez*, thou shalt have, let me see, ay, my fourth Spouse, she's a brave *Virago*; and Gad if I had not been something familiar with her already, I would venture my life for her.

4. Wom. Vile Wretch! think'st thou I will out-live this affront? Impious Villain! though thou hast no sense of Vertue or Honour left, thou shalt find I have.

D. Joh. Vertue and Honour ! There's nothing good or ill, but as it seems to each man's natural appetite, if they will consent freely. You must ravish friends : that's all I know, you must ravish.

1. Wom. Unheard of Villany ! Fly from this Hellish place.

Ant. Ladies, you shall fly, but we must ravish first.

D. Lop.

D. Lop. Yes, I assure you we must ravish——

4. *Wom.* No, Monster, I'll prevent you.　　　　[*Stabs her self.*

D. Ant. 'Sdeath, she's as good as her word.
The first time I e'r knew a Woman so.

D. Lop. Pox on't, she has prevented me; she's dead.

D. Joh. Say you so? well, go thy ways, thou wer't a Girl of
pretty parts, that's the truth on't; but I ne'r thought this had
been in thee.

2. *Wom.* These, sure, are Devils in the shape of men.

D. Joh. Now see my providence, if I had been marri'd to
none but her, I had been a Widdower.

1. *Wom.* O horror! horror! flie! flie!

6. *Wom.* No, I'll be reveng'd first on this barbarous Wretch.

D. Joh. Why look you, here's a Wench of mettle for you; go
ravish quickly——

6. *Wom.* Let's fly, and call for help, some in the street may
help us　　　　[*They all run off, crying, Help, murder, murder!*

D. Ant. Let 'em go, they are confin'd, they cann't get out.

D. Joh. It shall ne'r be said that a Woman went out of this
house *Remfecta*; but after that, 'twill be time for us to fly.

D. Lop. We have hir'd a Vessel, the Master is a brave Rogue
of my acquaintance; he has been a *Bandit.*

D. Ant. A brave honest wicked Fellow as heart can wish, I
have ravish'd, robb'd, and murder'd with him.

D. Joh. That's well. Hey, where are my Rogues? Hey!

Enter Servant and Jacomo.

Here, Sirra, do you send my Goods on Board.

Ant. My Man will direct you.　　　　[*Exit Servant.*

D. Joh. Come, Sirra, do you remove this Body to another
Room——

Jac. O horrid fact! what, another Murder! what shall I do?

D. Joh. Leave your complaints, you Dog; I'll send you after
her.

Jac. Oh! I shall be hang'd, I shall be hang'd.

D. Joh. Take her up, Rascal; or I'll cut your throat.

Jac. I will, Sir. Oh mercy upon me! I shall be hang'd ——

D. Joh. Now, Sirra, do you run into the streets, and force in the next Woman you meet, or I'll cut your Wind-pipe; and let no body out————

Jac. What hellish fact will he now commit?

D. Joh. Take her up, you Hen-hearted compassionate Rascal.

Jac. Heav'n! what will become of me? Oh! Oh ——

[*Carries her off.*

D. Joh. Now, Gentlemen, you shall see I'll be civil to you, you shall not ravish alone: indeed I am loath to meddle with mine old acquaintance, but if my Man can meet with a Woman I have not lain withall, I'll keep you company; let her be old or young, ugly or handsome, no matter.

D. Lop. Faith I will ever say, you are a well bred man.

D. Ant. A very civil person, a man of Honour.

Enter Servant, forcing in an ugly old Woman, who cries out.

D. Joh. This unlucky Rogue has made but a scurvy choice, but I'll keep my word. Come, Bawd, you must be ravish'd, Bawd.

Old. Wom. O murder! murder! help! help! I was never ravish'd in my life.

D. Joh. That I dare swear; but to show I am a very vigorous man, I'll begin with you. But, you Rascal, Jaccall, I'll make you Cater better next time.

Serv. Indeed, Sir, this was the first I met.

D. Joh. Come on, Beldam, thy face shall not protect thee.

Old Wom. Oh my Honour! my Honour! help, help, my Honour!

D. Joh. Come to our business.

Enter Jacomo.

Jac. O Sir! Sir! shift for your self; we shall all be hang'd: the house is beset. Oh what shall we do?

D. Joh. Away, Coward: were the King of *Spain*'s Army beleaguring leagu'ring us, it fhould not divert me from this Exploit.

D. Ant. Nor me.

D. Lop. Nor me : let's on.

D. Joh. Keep the doors faft, Sirra. Come on.

Jac. Oh what will become of me! Oh Heav'n! mercy on me!
Oh! Oh!   [*Exeunt.*

In *Man's habit, Enter* Maria, *and her Maid* Flora.

Mar. Thus I have abandon'd all my Fortune, and laid by
My Sex. Revenge for thee. Affift me now,
You Inftruments of Bloud, for my dear Brothers,
And for my much more dear *Octavio's* fake.
Where are my Bravo's?———

Flo. They have befet the Villains Houfe,
And he fhall ne'r come out alive.———

Mar. O let 'em fhow no more remorfe,
Than hungry Lions o'r their prey will.
How miferable am I made by that
Inhumane Monfter! No favage Beaft,
Wild Deferts e'r brought forth, provok'd
By all its hunger, and its natural rage,
Could yet have been fo cruel.
Oh my *Octavio*! whether art thou fled,
From the moft loving and moft wretched
Creature of her Sex? What Ages of delight
Each hour with thee brought forth!
How much, when I had thee, was all the world
Unenvi'd by me! Nay, I piti'd all my Sex,
That cou'd have nothing worth their care,
Since all the treafure of Mankind was mine.
Methought I cou'd look down on Queens, when he
Was with me : but now, compar'd to me,
How happy is the Wretched, whofe finews
Crack upon the mercilefs Engine
Of his torture? I live with greater torments then he dies.

Flo. Leave your complaints. Tears are no Sacrifice for
bloud.

        Mar.

Mar. Now my juſt grief to juſt revenge give place.
I am aſham'd of theſe ſoft Tears, till I've
Reveng'd thy horrid Murder. Oh that I could
Make the Villain linger out an Age in
Torments! But I will revel in his bloud: Oh
I could ſuck the laſt drop that warms the
Monſter's heart, that might inſpire me with
Such cruelty, as vile Man, with all his horrid
Arts of power, is yet a ſtranger to;
Then I might root out all his curſed Race.

Flo. I'll follow all your Fortunes, my dear Lady;
Had I ten thouſand lives, in this cauſe I'd
Venture one by one to my laſt ſtake.

Mar. Thou art my dear and faithful Creature;
Let not thy Fortunes thus be wrack'd with mine.
Be gone, and leave thy moſt unhappy Miſtris;
One that has miſeries enow to ſink the Sex.

Flo. I will not leave you, till death takes me from you.

Mar. O that I had been ſome poor loſt Mountain Girl,
Nurs'd up by Goats, or ſuckl'd by wild Beaſts,
Expos'd to all the rage of heats and killing colds.
I ne'r could have been aband on'd to ſuch fury.
More ſavage cruelty reigns in Cities,
Than ever yet in Deſarts among the
Moſt venomous Serpents, and remorſleſs
Ravenous Beaſts, could once be found.
So much has barb'rous Art debauch'd
Man's innocent Nature.

Flo. Lay by your tears, till your revenge be finiſh'd;
Then, then you may have leiſure to complain.

Mar. I will: 'tis bloud I now muſt ſpill, or
Loſe my own in th' attempt. But if I can
Have the fortune, with my own hand, to reach
The Dogs vile heart: I then ſhall die
Contented, and in the other World I'll
Torture him ſo, Devils ſhall learn of me to
bliſhe the Damn'd.

Flo. Let's to our Sacred Inſtruments of revenge.

Mar.

Mar. Come on : so just a cause would turn the
Vilest Ruffian to a Saint.   [*Exeunt.*
      [*Bravo's watch at* Don John's *house.*

Maria *and* Flora *re-enter.*

Mar. Come, friends, let once a Woman preach courage
To you, inspir'd by my just rage this Arm
Shall teach you wonders. I'll shew you now
What Love with just Revenge can do.
    1. *Brav.* We are so practis'd in the trade of death,
We need no teaching.
    Mar. There's Gold good store; if you dispatch the Dog,
I'll give you yet much more; if not,
If all the wealth I have can buy your lives,
I'll have 'em in stead of his.
    1. *Brav.* For half the Sum, I'd kill a Bishop at th' Altar.
      [*They retire.*

Enter Don John, Don Antonio, Don Lopez, Jacomo.

    D. Joh. Now we have finish'd our design; let's make a Salley,
and raise the Siege.
    D. Ant. Jacomo, do you lead the Van.
    D. Lop. Lead on, Jacomo, or we are sure to lose you; you are
not good at bringing up the Rear.
    Jac. Nay, good Gentlemen, I know my self better than to
take place of Men of Quality, especially upon this occasion.
    D. Joh. Sirra, go on: I'll prick him forward. Remember, if
you do not fight, I am behind you.
    Jac. Oh Heav'n! Oh Jacomo! what will become of thy dear
person? Is this your Courage to put me forward, to what you
dare not meet your selves?
    D. Joh. No words, Rogue, on, on, I say ———
    Jac. O I shall be murder'd! murder'd! Oh! Oh!———
    D. Joh. On, on, you Dog.
    Jac. Inhumane Master! It must be so! Heav'n have mercy on
my better part.
      Enter

Enter Maria.

Mar. Fall on, fall on, that's the Villain! Have at you, Dog---
D. Joh. Courage, *Jacomo.*

      [*They fight, and are driven off, but*
      Maria *and* Flora *remain.*

Jac. Oh! Oh!
Mar. Oh cowardly Villains! the Traitor will escape their
hands. Oh Dogs! more feeble than the feeblest of our Sex
Let's after him, and try our strength.

Enter Don John.

He is return'd —— fall on.
    D. Joh. Ha! must I encounter Boys?
    Flo. Oh I am slain———   [*Kills* Flora.
    Mar. At thy heart, base Villain.   [Don John *disarms* Maria.
    D. Joh. There, take your Sword; I'll not nip Roguery in the
bud; thou may'st live to be as wicked as my self.
    Mar. Poor *Flora!* But, Dog, I'll be reveng'd on thee yet ere
I die.   [*Exit.*

Enter Don Lopez, Don Antonio, Jacomo.

Jac. What! no thanks! no reward!
    D. Joh. What's the matter, Sirra?
    Jac. What, no acknowledgment? you are but an ungrateful
man, let me tell you that, to treat a man of my prowess thus.
    D. Joh. What has your valour done?
    Jac. Nothing, nothing; sav'd your life onely, that's all: but
men of valour are nothing now adays. 'Tis an ungrateful Age.
I fought like a *Hero*
    D. Ant. Call'd a Stag at Bay.
    D. Lop. You can fight, when there's no way of escape, with-
out it.
    Jac. Oh! what's here! another murder! fly, fly; we shall be
hang'd.

                                       D. Joh.

D. Joh. Come on! let's now to Sea to try our fortunes.

Jac. Ay, make haste; I've laid Horses, and will shift by Land. Farewell, Sir; a good Voyage——

D. Joh. I will murder you, if you refuse to go to Sea——

Jac. O, good Sir, consider, do but consider; I am so Sea-sick always: that wicked Element does not agree with me.

D. Joh. Dare you dispute! go on, I say.

Jac. O, good Sir, think, think a little; the merciless Waves will never consider a man of parts: besides, Sir, I can swim no more than I can fly.

D. Joh. I'll leave you dead upon the place, if you refuse.

Jac. O Sir, on my knees I beg you'll let me stay. I am the last of all my Family; my Race will fail, if I should fail.

D. Joh. Damn your Race ——

D. Ant. Do not we venture with you?

Jac. You have nothing but your lives to venture, but I have a whole Family to save; I think upon Posterity. Besides, Gentlemen, I can look for no safety in such wicked company.

D. Joh. I'll kill the Villain. His fear will else betray us.

Jac. O hold! hold! for Heav'ns sake hold ——

       [*Ghost of* Don John's *Father rises.*

Ghost. Hold! hold!

Jac. Ay, hold, hold. Oh Heav'n! your Father's Ghost; a Ghost! a Ghost! Oh! Oh!   [*Falls down and roars.*

D. Joh. 'Sdeath! what's here? my Father alive!

Ghost. No, no; inhumane Murderer, I am dead.

D. Joh. That's well; I was afraid the old Gentleman had come for his Estate again; if you wou'd have that, 'tis too late; 'tis spent ——

Ghost. Monster! behold these wounds.

D. Joh. I do; they were well meant, and well perform'd, I see.

D. Ant. This is strange! how I am amaz'd!

D. Lop. Unheard of Wonder! ——

Ghost. Repent, repent of all thy villanies; My clamorous blood to Heav'n for vengeance cries.

      F   Heav'n

Heav'n will pour out his judgments on you all ;
Hell gapes for you, for you each Fiend does call,
And hourly waits your unrepenting fall.
You with eternal horrours they'l torment,
Except of all your crimes you suddenly repent. *[Ghost sinks.*

Jac. Oh! Oh! Heav'n deliver me from these Monsters.

D. Joh. Farewell, thou art a foolish Ghost ; Repent, quoth he! what could this mean? our senses are all in a mist sure.

D. Ant. They are not, 'twas a Ghost.

D. Lop. I ne'r believ'd those foolish Tales before.

D. Joh. Come, 'tis no matter ; let it be what it will, it must be natural ——

D. Ant. And Nature is unalterable in us too.

D. Joh. 'Tis true, the nature of a Ghost cannot change ours.

D. Lop. It was a silly Ghost, and I'll no sooner take his word than a Whores.

D. Joh. Thou art in the right. Come, Fool, Fool, rise ; the Ghost is gone.

Jac. Oh! I die, I die ; pray let me die in quiet.

D. Ant. Oh! if he be dying, take him up ; we'll give him burial in the Sea. Come on.

Jac. Hold, hold, Gentlemen ; bury me not till I am dead, I beseech you ———

D. Joh. If you be not, Sirra, I'll run you through.

Jac. Hold, hold, Sir, I'll go, I'll go ——

D. Lop. }
D. Ant. } Let's on.

D. Joh. Should all the Bugbears Cowards feign appear,
I would urge on without one thought of fear.

D. Ant. And I.

D. Lop. And I. ———   *[Exeunt omnes.*

ACT

ACT III.

Enter Don John, Don Lopez, Don Antonio, Jacomo,
Captain of the Ship, Master and Sailors.

Mist. MErcy upon us! what sudden dreadful storm is this? we are all lost; we shall split upon the Rocks. Loof, loof——

Jac. Oh! Oh! Mercy! Oh I was afraid of this! See what your wickedness has brought me to? Mercy! mercy!

D. Joh. Take away thy Cowardly face, it offends me, Rascal.

Capt. Such dreadful claps of Thunder I never yet remember'd.

D. Joh. Let the Clowds roar on, and vomit all their Sulphur out, they ne'r shall fright me. ——

D. Ant. These are the Squibs and Crackers of the Sky.

D. Lop. Fire on, fire on; we are unmov'd.

Capt. The Heav'ns are all on fire; these unheard of Prodigies amaze me.

D. Joh. Can you, that have stood so many Cannons, be frighted at the farting and the belching of a Clowd?

Mist. Bless me, Captain! six of our Foremast men are even now struck dead with Lightning.

Sail. O that clap has rent our Masts in sunder.

Jac. O we are lost! You can swim, Sir; pray save me, Sir, for my own and Family's sake. ——

D. Joh. Toss these cowardly Rogues over-board. Captain, Courage! let the Heav'ns do their worst, 'tis but drowning at last.

Jac. But—— in the name of Heav'n, but drowning, quoth he; your drowning will prepare you for burning, though Oh, Oh, Oh ——

Sail. Captain, Captain, the Ship's on fire in the Forecastle——;

Capt. All hands to work upon the Forecastle. Heav'n! how it blazes already! —— [*Exit Captain.*

Jac. Oh! Oh! we burn, we drown, we sink, Oh! we perish, we are lost, we are lost. Oh, Oh, Oh ——

F 2   *Mist.*

Mast. O horrid Apparitions! Devils stand and guard the fire, and will not suffer us to quench it. We are lost.

Enter Captain.

Capt. In all the dangers I have been, such horrors I never knew; I am quite unmann'd.

D. Lop. A man and fear: 'tis but dying at last.

D. Joh. I never yet could know what that foolish thing Fear is.

Capt. Help, help, the fire increases. What horrid sights are these? where e'r I turn me, fearful Spirits appear.

[*Exeunt Captain and Sailors.*

D. Joh. Let's into the Boat, and with our Swords keep out all others.

D. Ant. While they are busie 'bout the fire we may 'scape.

D. Lop. If we get from hence, we certainly shall perish on the Rocks ——

D. Joh. I warrant you ——

Jac. O good Gentlemen, let us shift for our selves, and let the rest burn, or drown, and be damn'd and they will.

D. Joh. No, you have been often leaving me: now shall be the time we'll part. Farewell.

Jac. Oh! I'll stand by you while I live. Oh the Devil, the Devil! What horrors do I feel? Oh I am kill'd, I am dead!

[*A Thunder-clap strikes* Don John
and Jacomo *down.*

D. Joh. 'Sdeath! why this to me? you paltry foolish bug-bear Thunder, am I the mark of your senseless rage?

D. Lop. Nothing but accident. Let's leap into the Boat.

D. Ant. The Sailors all make towards us; they'll in and sink it.

D. Joh. Sirra, if you come on, you run upon my Sword.

Jac. O cruel Tyrant! I burn, I drown, I sink! Oh I die, I am lost.

Capt. All shift aboard; we perish, we are lost.

Mast. All lost, all lost.

[*A great shreik, they all leap over-board.*
Enter

Enter an old Hermit.

Her. This fourty years I've liv'd in this neigbouring **Cave,** and from thefe dreadful Cliffs which are always beaten by the foaming Surges of the Sea; beheld the Ocean in its wildeft rage, and ne'r yet faw a ftorm fo dreadful: fuch horrid flaſhes of lightning, and fuch claps of thunder, never were in my remembrance. Yon Ship is all on fire, and the poor miferable Wretches muft all perifh. The dreadful object melts my heart, and brings a floud of tears into my eyes: It is prodigious, for on the fudden, all the Heavens are clear again, and the inraged Sea is become more patient.

Enter Don Francifco.

D. Fran. Oh Father, have you not been frighted at this prodigious ftorm, and at yon dreadful fpectacle?

Herm. No man that has an apprehenfion, but wou'd have been mov'd with horrour.

D. Franc. 'Twas the moft violent Tempeft I ever faw. Hold, yonder are fome coming in a fmall Veffel, and muft neceffarily fplit upon the Rock; I'll go and help to fuccour 'em.

Herm. Here are fome this way, juft come in a fmall Boat: Co you to thofe, and thefe I will affift——

D. Fran. I'll hafte to their relief —— [*Exit* Don Fran.

Herm. Hah! thefe are come fafe to Land, three men, goodly men they feem to be; I am bound in charity to ferve them: they come towards me.

Enter Don John, Don Antonio, *and* Don Lopez.

D. Joh. Much ado we are fafe, but my Man's loft; pox on him, I fhall mifs the Fool, it was a neceffary Blockhead.

D. Ant. But you have loft your Goods, which were more neceffary.

D. Lop. Our Jewels and Money we have all about us.

D. Joh. It makes me laugh to think, how the Fools we left
behind

behind were puzzl'd which death to chuse, burning or drowning———

D. Ant. But how shall we dispose of our selves, we are plaguy wet and cold. Hah! what old Fool is that?

D. Lop. It is an Hermit, a fellow of mighty Beard and Sanctity.

D. Joh. I know not what Sanctity he may have, but he has Beard enough to make an Owls Nest, or stuff a Saddle with.

Herm. Gentlemen, I see you are shipwrack'd, and in distress; and my Function obliges me in charity to succour you in what I may.

D. Ant. Alas! what canst thou help us to? dost thou know of ever a house near hand, where we may be furnished with some necessaries?

Herm. On the other side of this vast Rock, there is a fertile and a pleasant Valley, where one *Don Francisco*, a rich and hospitable man, has a sweet Dwelling; he will entertain you nobly: He's gone to assist some shipwrack'd persons, and will be here presently. In the mean time, what my poor Cave can afford, you shall be welcome to.

D. Lop. What can that afford? you oblige your self to fasting and abstinence ———

Herm. I have studi'd Physick for the relief of needy people, and I have some Cordials which will refresh you; I'll bring one to you——— [*Exit Hermit.*

D. Joh. A good civil old Hipocrite: but this is a pleasant kind of Religion, that obliges 'em to nastiness and want of meat. I'll ha' none on't.———

D. Ant. No, nor of any other, to my knowledge.

Enter Hermit with a Cordial.

Herm. Gentlemen, pray taste of this Vial, it will comfort your cold stomachs.

D. Joh. Ha! 'tis excellent 'faith. Let it go round.

Herm. Heav'n bless it to you.

D. Lop. Ha! it warms.

D. Ant. Thank thee, thou art a very honest old fellow i'faith.

D. Joh. I see thou art very civil; but you must supply us

with

with one neceſſary more; a very neceſſary thing, and very re-
freſhing.

Her.n. What's that, *Sir?*

D. Joh. It is a Whore, a fine young buxom Whore.

D. Ant.
D. Lop. } A Whore, Old man, a Whore.

Herm. Bleſs me, are you Men or Devils ?——

D. Joh. Men, men, and men of luſt and vigour. Pre'thee, old
Sot, leave thy prating, and help me to a Strumpet, a fine ſala-
cious Strumpet; I know you Zealots have enough of 'em. Women love your godly Whore-maſters.

Herm. O Monſters of impiety! are you ſo lately ſcap'd the
wrath of Heaven, thus to provoke it ?

D. Ant. How! by following the Dictates of Nature, who can
do otherwiſe?

D. Lop. All our actions are neceſſitated, none command their
own wills.

Herm. Oh horrid blaſphemy! would you lay your dreadful
and unheard of Vices upon Heaven? No, ill men, that has
given you free-will to good.

D. Joh. I find thou retir'ſt here, and never readſt or thinkſt.
Can that blind faculty the Will be free,
When it depends upon the Underſtanding?
Which argues firſt before the Will can chuſe;
And the laſt Dictate of the Judgment ſways
The Will, as in a Balance, the laſt Weight
Put in the Scale, lifts up the other end,
And with the ſame Neceſſity.

Herm. But fooliſh men and ſinners act againſt
Their Underſtandings, which inform 'em better.

D. Ant. None willingly do any thing againſt the laſt
Dictates of their Judgments, whatſoe'r men do,
Their preſent opinions lead 'em to.

D. Lop. As fools that are afraid of ſin, are by the thought
Of preſent pleaſure, or ſome other reaſon,
Neceſſarily byaſs'd to purſue
The opinion they are of at that moment.

Herm. The Underſtanding yet is free, and might perſwade 'em
better.

D. Joh.

D. Joh. The Underſtanding never can be free;
For what we underſtand, ſpite of our ſelves we do:
All objects are ready form'd and plac'd
To our hands; and theſe the Senſes to the Mind convey,
And as thoſe repreſent them, this muſt judge:
How can the Will be free, when the Underſtanding,
On which the Will depends, cannot be ſo.

Herm. Lay by your devilliſh Philoſophy, and change the dangerous and deſtructive courſe of your lewd lives.

D. Ant. Change our natures? Go bid a Blackamore be white, we follow our Conſtitutions, which we did not give our ſelves.

D. Lop. What we are, we are by Nature, our reaſon tells us we muſt follow that.

D. Joh. Our Conſtitutions tell us one thing, and yours another; and which muſt we obey? If we be bad, 'tis Nature's fault that made us ſo.

Herm. Farewell. I dare no longer hear your impious diſcourſe. Such harden'd Wretches I ne'r heard of yet.

[*Exit Hermit.*

D. Ant. Farewell, old Fool.

D. Joh. Thus Sots condemn what they can never anſwer.

Enter Don Franciſco.

This I believe is *Franciſco*, whom he ſpoke of; if he has but a handſome Wife, or Daughters, we are happy.

D. Lop. Sir, we are ſhipwrack'd men, and if you can direct us to a place, where we may be furniſh'd with ſome neceſſaries, you will oblige us ——

D. Franc. Gentlemen, I have a Houſe hard by, you ſhall be welcome to it: I even now endeavoured to ſuccour a Youth and beauteous Woman, who, with two Sailors, in a Boat, were driven towards theſe Rocks, but were forc'd back again, and, I fear, are loſt by this time. I deſire nothing more, than to aſſiſt men in extremes, and am o'rjoy'd at the opportunity of ſerving you.

D. Joh. We thank you.

D. Fran. You ſhall command my Houſe as long as you pleaſe:

Vſee

I see you are Cavaliers, and hope you will bear with some inconvenience. I have two young, and, though I say it, handsome Daughters, who are, to morrow morning to be marri'd; the Solemnity will bring much company together, which, I fear, may incommode my house and you ——

D. Ant. You pose us with this kindness.

D. Joh. What ever pleases you, cannot be inconvenient to us.

D. Lop. On the contrary, we shall be glad to assist you at the Ceremony, and help to make up the joyful *Chorus*.

D. Fran. You shall command my house and me; I'll shew you the way to it.

D. Joh. Your humble Servant. We'll follow you.

         ⟨ *Exit* Don Francisco.

This is an admirable adventure.
He has Daughters, Boys, and to be marri'd too:
If they have been so foolish, to preserve those
Toys, they call *Maidenheads*; their senseless
Husbands shall not be troubled with them:
I'll ease them of those. Pox, what should those dull
Drudging Animals, call'd Husbands, do with such **Treasures**:
No, they are for honest Whore-masters, Boys.

D. Ant. Well said, *Don*; we will not be wanting in our endeavours to succeed you.

D. Lop. To you alone we must give place. Allons. [*Exeunt.*

Enter Hermit, Maria *in Man's habit, and* Leonora.

Herm. Heaven be prais'd, you are safely now on Land.
Mar. We thank you, reverend Father, for your assistance.
Leon. We never shall forget the obligation.
Herm. I am happy to be so good an Instrument.
Leon. We follow'd a Vessel, which we saw fir'd with Lightning, and we fear that none of 'em escap'd.
Mar. I hope the Villain I pursue has scap'd. I would not be reveng'd by Heaven, but my own hand; or, if not by that, by the Hangman's.
Leon. Did any come to Land? for I most nearly am concern'd

        G   for

or one; the grief for whom, if he be loſt, will ſoon, I fear, deſtroy me.

Herm. Here were three of that company came ſafe to Land; but ſuch impious Wretches, as did not deſerve to eſcape, and ſuch as no vertuous perſon can be concern'd for, ſure; I was ſtiff with fear and horrour when I heard 'em talk.

Mar. Three, ſay you?

Leon. By this ſad deſcription it muſt be *Don John*, and his two wicked Aſſociates; I am aſham'd to confeſs the tenderneſs I have for him. Why ſhould I love that Wretch? Oh my too violent paſſion hurries me I know not whether! into what fearful dangerous Labyrinths of miſery will it conduct me?

Mar. Were they Gentlemen?

Herm. By their out-ſides they ſeem'd ſo, but their in-ſides declar'd them Devils.

Mar. Heaven! it muſt be the Villain and his barbarous Companions. They are reſerv'd for my revenge:
Aſſiſt me, Heaven, in that juſt cauſe.
Oh, Villain, Villain! inhumane Villain!
Each minute is, me-thinks, a tedious Age,
Till I have dipt my hands in thy hearts bloud.

Herm. You ſeem o'r-joy'd at the news of their ſafe arrival: Can any have a kindneſs for ſuch diſſolute abandon'd Atheiſts?

Mar. No; 'tis revenge that I perſue againſt the baſeſt of all Villains.

Herm. Have a care; Revenge is Heavens, and muſt not be uſurp'd by Mortals.

Mar. Mine is revenge for Rapes and cruel murders, and thoſe Heaven leaves to Earth to puniſh.

Herm. They are horrid crimes, but Magiſtrates muſt puniſh them.

Leon. What do I hear? were he the baſeſt of all men, my love is ſo head-ſtrong and ſo wild within me, I muſt endeavour to preſerve him, or deſtroy my ſelf: to what deplorable condition am I fall'n? what Chains are theſe that hold me? Oh that I could break them! and yet I wou'd not if I cou'd; Oh my heart!

Herm. They are gon to one *Don Franciſco's* houſe, that Road

will

will bring you to it; 'tis on the other side of this Rock, in a pleasant Valley. I have not stirr'd these fourty years from these small bounds, or I wou'd give him notice what Devils he harbours in his house. You will do well to do it.

Jac. (*within*) Help, help, murder! I am drown'd, I am dead; Help, help!

Herm. Hah! what voice is that? I must assist him——

Mar. Father, farewell. Come, Madam, will you go to this house? Now, Monster, for my revenge.

Leon. I will; but for different ends we go; 'Tis Love conducts me, but Revenge brings you.

[*Exeunt* Maria, Leonora.

Jac. Oh help, help! I sink, I sink!

Herm. Poor man, sure he is almost drown'd.

Jac. No, not yet; I have onely drunk something too much of a scurvy unpleasant Liquor.

Herm. Reach me your hand —— [*Pulls him out.*

Jac. Ay, and my heart too; Oh! Oh! Sir, a thousand thanks to you: I vow to Gad, y'are a very civil person, and, as I am an honest man, have done me the greatest kindness in the world, next to the piece of the Mast which I floated upon, which I must ever love and honour; I am sorry it swam away, I wou'd have preserv'd it, and hung it up in the Seat of our antient Family.

Herm. Thank Heaven for your deliverance, and leave such vain thoughts.

Jac. I do with all my heart; but I am not setled enough to say my prayers yet: pray, Father, do you for me; 'tis nothing with you, you are us'd to it, it is your Trade.

Herm. Away, vain man; you speak as if you had drunk too deeply of another Liquor than Sea-water.

Jac. No, I have not, but I wou'd fain: Where may a man light of a good Glass of Wine? I would gladly have an Antidote to my Poison. Methinks, Pah! these Fishes have but a scurvy time; I am sure they have very ill-drinking.

Herm. Farewell, and learn more devotion and thankfulness to Heav'n —— [*Exit Hermit.*

Jac. Ha! 'tis uncivilly done to leave a man in a strange Country.

Bu

But these *Hermits* have no breeding. Poor *Jacomo*, Dear *Jacomo*, how I love thy person, how glad am I to see thee safe? for I swear, I think thou art as honest a fellow as e'r I met with. Well, farewell, thou wicked Element; if ever I trust thee again———— Well, Haddocks, I defie you, you shall have none of me, no, not a Collop; no, no, I will be eaten by Worms, as all my Ancestors have been. It Heaven will but preserve me from the Monsters of the Land, my Master and his two Companions (who, I hope, are drown'd) I'll preserve my self from those of the Sea. Let me see, here is a path———— this must lead to some house. I'll go, for I am plaguy sick with this Salt-water. Pah———— [*Exit* Jacomo.

Enter Clara *and* Flavia, *with her two Maids.*

Clar. Oh, *Flavia*, this will be our last happy night, to morrow is our Execution day; we must marry.

Flav. Ay, *Clara*, we are condemn'd without reprieve. 'Tis better to live as we have done, kept from all men, than for each to be confin'd to one, whom yet we never saw, and a thousand to one shall never like.

Clar. Out on't, a *Spanish* Wife has a worse life than a coop'd Chicken.

Flan. A singing Bird in a Cage is a Princely creature, compar'd to that poor Animal, call'd a Wife, here.

Clar. Birds are made tame by being cag'd, but Women grow wild by confinement, and that, I fear, my Husband will find to his cost.

Flav. None live pleasantly here, but those who should be miserable, Strumpets: They can choose their Mates, but we must be like Slaves condemn'd to the Gallies; we have not liberty to sell our Selves, or venture one throw for our freedom.

Clar. O that we were in *England*! there, they say, a Lady may choose a Footman, and run away with him, if she likes him, and no dishonour to the Family.

Flav. That's because the Families are so very Honourable, that nothing can touch them: there Wives run and ramble whither and with whom they please, and defie all censure.

Clar.

Clar. Ay, and a jealous Husband is a more monftrous Creature there, than a Wittall here, and wou'd be more pointed at:
They fay, if a man be jealous there, the women will all joyn and
pull him to pieces.

Flav. Oh happy Countrey! we ne'r touch money, there the
Wives can fpend their Husbands Eftates for 'em. Oh blefs'd
Countrey!

Clar. Ay, there, they fay, the Husbands are the prettieft civil
eafie good natur'd indifferent perfons in the whole world; they
ne'r mind what their Wives do, not they.

Flav. Nay, they fay, they love thofe men beft that are kindeft
to their Wives. Good men! poor hearts. And here, if an honeft
Gentleman offers a Wife a civility by the By, our bloudy butch-
erly Husbands are cutting of throats prefently ———

Clar. Oh that we had thofe frank civil *Englifh-men*, inftead
of our grave dull furly *Spanifh* Blockheads, whofe greateft honour lies, in preferving their Beards and Foreheads inviolable.

Flav. In *England*, if a Husband and Wife like not one another, they draw two feveral ways, and make no bones on't,
while the Husband treats his Miftris openly in his Glafs-Coach;
the Wife, for decency's fake, puts on her Vizar, and whips away
in a Hackney with a Gallant, and no harm done.

Clar. Though, of late, 'tis as unfafhionable for a Husband to
love his Wife there, as 'tis here, yet 'tis fafhionable for her to
love fome body elfe, and that's fomething.

Flav. Nay, they fay, Gentlemen will keep company with a
Cuckold there, as foon as another man, and ne'r wonder at him.

Clar. Oh happy Countrey! there a Woman may chufe for her
felf, and none will into the Trap of Matrimony, unlefs fhe likes
the Bait; but here we are tumbl'd headlong and blindfold into it.

Flav. We are us'd as they ufe Hawks, never unhooded, or
whiftled off, till they are juft upon the Quarry.

Clar. And 'tis for others, not our felves, we fly too.

Flav. No more, this does but put us in mind of our mifery.

Clar. It does fo: but prethee let's be merry one night, to morrow is our laft. Farewell all happinefs.

Flav. O that this happy day would laft our lives-time. But
prethee,

prethee, my Dear, let's have thy Song, and divert our selves as well as we can in the mean time.

Clar. 'Tis a little too wanton.

Flav. Prethee let's be a little wanton this evening, to morrow we must take our leaves on't.

Clar. Come on then ; our Maids shall joyn in the *Chorus :* Here they are.

SONG.

Woman who is by Nature wild,
   Dull bearded men incloses ;
Of Nature's freedom we're beguil'd
   By Laws which man imposes :
Who still himself continues free,
Yet we poor Slaves must fetter'd be.

Chor. Ashame on the Curse
      Of, For better for worse ;
   'Tis a vile imposition on Nature :
      For Women should change,
      And have freedom to range,
   Like to every other wild Creature.

So gay a thing was ne'r design'd.
   To be restrain'd from roving ;
Heav'n meant so changeable a mind
   Should have its change in loving.
By cunning we could make men smart,
But they by strength o'rcome our Art.

Chor. Ashame on the Curse
      Of, For, &c.

How happy is the Village Maid,
   Whom onely Love can fetter ;
By foolish Honour ne'r betray'd,
   She serves a Pow'r much greater :

That

That lawful Prince the wisest rules,
Th'Usurper Honour rules but Fools.

Chor. A shame on the Curse
   'Of, For, &c.

Let us resume our antient right,
   Make man at distance wonder;
Though he victorious be in fight,
   In love we'll keep him under.
War and Ambition hence be hurl'd,
Let Love and Beauty rule the World.

Chor. A shame on the Curse
   Of, For better, &c.

Flav. Oh, dear *Clara*, that this were true! But now let's home, our Father will miss us.

Clar. No, he's walk'd abroad with the three Shipwrack'd Gentlemen.

Flav. They're proper handsome Gentlemen; but the chief, whom they call *Don John*, exceeds the rest.

Clar. I never saw a finer person; pray Heaven either of our Husbands prove as good.

Flav. Do not name 'em. Let the Maids go home, and if my Father be there, let him know we are here.   [*Exit Maids.*

Clar. In the mean time, if he be thereabouts, do you go down that Walk, and I'll go this way, and perhaps one of us shall light on him.

Flav. Agreed.   [*Exit ambo.*

Enter Don John, Don Lopez, Don Antonio.

D. Joh. Where have you left the Old man, *Don Francisco?*

D. Lop. He's very busie at home, seeing all things prepar'd for his Daughters Weddings to morrow.

D. Joh. His Daughters are gone this way: if you have any
                                             friendship

friendſhip for me, go and watch the Old man; and if he offers
to come towards us, divert him, that I may have freedom to at-
tack his Daughters.

D. Ant. You may be ſure of us, that have ſerv'd you with our
lives; beſides, the juſtice of this cauſe will make us ſerve you.
Adieu.   [*Exeunt* Don Lop. Don. Ant.

D. Joh. Now for my Virgins. Aſſiſt me, Love. Fools, you ſhall
have no Maiden-heads to morrow-night. Husbands have
Maiden-heads! no, no — poor ſneaking Fools.

Enter Jacomo.

Jac. I have loſt my way, I think I ſhall never find this houſe:
But I ſhall never think my ſelf out of my way, unleſs I meet my
impious Maſter; Heaven grant he be drown'd.

D. Joh. How now, Raſcal, are you alive?

Jac. Oh Heaven! he's here. Why was this lewd Creature
ſav'd? I am in a worſe condition than ever; now I have ſcap'd
drowning, he brings hanging freſh into my memory.

D. Joh. What mute, Sirra?

Jac. Sir, I am no more your Servant, you parted with me, I
thank you, Sir, I am beholding to you: Farewell, good Sir, I
am my own man now——

D. Joh. No: though you are a Rogue, you are a neceſſary
Rogue, and I'll not part with you.

Jac. I muſt be gone, I dare not venture further with you.

D. Joh. Sirra, do you know me, and dare you ſay this to me?
have at your Guts, I will rip you from the Navel to the Chin.

Jac. O good Sir, ho'd, hold. He has got me in his clutches, I
ſhall never get looſe —— Oh! Oh!———

D. Joh. Come, Dog, follow me cloſe, ſtinking Raſcal.

Jac. I am too well pick'l'd in the Salt-water to ſtink, I thank
you, I ſhall keep a great while. But you were a very generous
man, to leave a Gentleman, your Friend, in danger, as you did
me. I have reaſon to follow you: but if I ſerve you not in your
kind, then am I a ſows'd Sturgeon.

D. Joh. Follow me, Sirra; I ſee a Lady.

Jac. Are you ſo fierce already?

Enter

Enter Clara, *singing,* A ſhame on the Curſe, &c.

Clar. Ha ! this is the Stranger ;
What makes him here ?

D. Joh. A delicate Creature. Ha ! this is the Lady.
How happy am I to meet you here━━━

Clar. What mean you, Sir ?

D. Joh. I was undone enough before, with ſeeing your Picture
in the Gallery ; but I ſee you have more Excellencies than Beauty, your Voice needed not have conſpir'd with that to ruine
me.

Clar. Have you ſeen my Picture ?

D. Joh. And lov'd it above all things I ever ſaw, but the Ori-
ginal. I am loſt beyond redemption, unleſs you can pity me.

Jac. (*aſide*) He has been loſt a hundred times, but he always
finds himſelf again ━━ and me too ; a pox on him.

D. Joh. When Love had taken too faſt hold on me, ever to
let me go, I too late found you were to morrow to be marri'd.

Clar. Yes, I am condemn'd to one I never ſaw, and you are
come to railly me and my misfortunes.

Jac. Ah, Madam, ſay not ſo, my Maſter is always in earneſt.

D. Joh. So much I am in earneſt now, that if you have no way
to break this marriage off, and pity me, I ſoon ſhall repent I ever
came to Land ; I ſhall ſuffer a worſe wrack upon the Shoar, here
I ſhall linger out my life in the worſt of pains, deſpairing Love ;
there, I ſhould have periſh'd quickly ━━━

Jac. Ah poor man ! he's in a deſperate condition, I pity him
with all my heart━━

D. Joh. Peace, Raſcal. Madam, this is the onely opportunity
I am like to have ; Give me leave to improve it.

Clar. Sure, Sir, you cannot be in earneſt.

D. Joh. If all the Oaths under the Sun can convince you, Madam, I ſwear━━

Jac. O Sir, Sir, have a care of ſwearing, for fear you ſhould,
once in your life, be forſworn━━

D. Joh. Peace, Dog, or I ſhall ſlit your Wind-pipe.

Jac. Nay, I know if he be forſworn, 'tis the firſt time, that's certain.

Clar. But, Sir, if you be in earneſt, and I had an inclination, 'Tis impoſſible to bring it about, my Father has diſpos'd of me.

D. Joh. Diſpoſe of your ſelf, I'll do well enough with him, and my Fortune and Quality are too great for him, for whom you are intended, to diſpute with me.

Clar. If this be true, wou'd you win a Woman at firſt ſight?

D. Joh. Madam, this is like to be the firſt and laſt; to morrow is the fatal day that will undo me.

Jac. Courage, *Don*, matters go well.

Clar. Nay, I had rather have a Peaſant of my own chooſing, than an Emperor of another's. He is a handſome Gentleman, and ſeems to be of quality: Oh that he could rid me of my intended ſlavery. [*Aſide.*

Sir, talk not of impoſſible things; for could I wiſh this, my Father's Honour will not ſuffer him to diſpenſe wtih his promiſe.

D. Joh. I'll carry you beyond his power, and your intended Husband's too.

Clar. It cannot be; but I muſt leave you, I dare not be ſeen with you ———

D. Joh. Remember the ſhort time you have to think on this: will you let me periſh without relief? if you will have pity on a wretched man, I have a Prieſt in my company, I'll marry you, and we'll find means to fly early in the morning, before the houſe are ſtirring.

Clar. I confeſs I am to be condemn'd to a Slavery, that nothing can be worſe; yet this were a raſh attempt.

D. Joh. If you will not conſent to my juſt deſires, I am reſolv'd to kill my ſelf, and fall a Sacrifice to your diſdain. Speak, ſpeak my doom ———. [*Holds his Sword to his breaſt.*

Clar. Hold, hold ———

Jac. Ay, hold, hold: poor fooliſh Woman, ſhe ſhou'd not need to bid him hold.

Clar. I'll find a means this night to ſpeak with you alone; but I fear this is but for your diverſion.

Jac. Yes, 'tis for diverſion indeed; the common diverſion of all the world.

D. Joh.

D. Joh. By all that's great and good, my intentions are honourable.

Clar. Farewell, Sir, I dare not stay longer.

D. Joh. Will you keep your word, Madam?

Jac. You'll keep yours, no doubt ————

Clar. I will, any thing rather than marry one I cannot love, as I can no man of another's choosing.

D. Joh. Remember, Madam, I perish if you do not; I have onely one thing to say, Keep this Secret from your Sister, till we have effected it; I'll give you sufficient reason for what I say.

[*Exit* Clar.

Victoria, Victoria; I have her fast, she's my own.

Jac. You are a hopeful man, you may come to good in time.

Enter Flavia.

D. Joh. Here is the other Sister; have at her.

Jac. Why, Sir, Sir; have you no conscience? Will not one at once serve your turn?

D. Joh. Stand by, Fool. Let me see, you are the Lady.

Flav. What say you, Sir?

D. Joh. You have lately taken up a stray heart of mine, I hope you do not intend to detain it, without giving me your own in exchange.

Flav. I a heart of yours? since when good Sir? you were but this day shipwrack'd on this Coast, and never saw my face before.

D. Joh. I saw your Picture, and I saw your motion, both so charming, I could not resist them; but now I have a nearer view, I see plainly I am lost.

Flav. A goodly handsome man! but what can this mean?

D. Joh. Such killing Beauties I ne'r saw before; my heart is irrevocably gone.

Flav. Whether is it gone, Sir? I assure you I have no such thing about me, that I know of.

D. Joh. Ah, Madam, if you wou'd give me leave to search you, I should find it in some little corner about you, that shall be nameless.

Flav. It cannot be about me, I have none but my own, and that

H 3   that

that I must part with to morrow to I know not whom.

D. Joh. If the most violent love that man e'r knew can e'r deserve that treasure, it is mine ; if you give that away, you lose the truest Lover that e'r languish'd yet.

Jac. What can be the end of this ? Sure Bloud must follow this dishonour of the Family, and I unfortunate, shall have my throat cut for company.

Flav. Do you know where you are?

D. Joh. Yes, Madam, in *Spain*, where opportunities are very scarce, and those that are wise make use of 'em as soon as they have 'em.

Flav. You have a mind to divert your self; but I must leave you, I am dispos'd to be more serious.

D. Joh. Madam, I swear by all——

Jac. Hold, hold ; will you be forsworn again?

D. Joh. Peace, Villain, I shall cut that tongue out.

Flav. Farwell, I cannot stay.   [*Exit* Flavia.

D. Joh. I'll not leave her ; I'll thaw her, if she were Ice, before I have done with her.

Jac. There is no end of this lewdness. Well, I must be kill'd or hang'd once for all, and there's an end on't.   [*Exeunt.*

Enter Maria *and* Leonora.

Leon. I am faint with what I suffer'd at Sea, and with my wandring since ; let us repose a little, we shall not find this house to night.

Mar. I ne'r shall rest till I have found *Don Francisco's* house ; but I'll sit down a while.

Leon. I hope he will not find it, till I have found means to give *Don John* warning of his cruel intentions : I would save his life, who, I fear, would not do that for me. But in the miserable case that I am in, if he denies his love, death would be the welcom'st thing on earth to me.

Mar. Oh my *Octavio* ! how does the loss of thee perplex me with despair ! the honour of Mankind is gone with thee. Why do I whine? grief shall no longer usurp the place of my revenge. How could I gnaw the Monster's heart, Villain ! I'll be with you.

When

When I have reveng'd my dear *Octavio's* loss, I then shall die contented.

Enter Don Lopez *and* Don Antonio.

D. Lop. Th'old man's safe; I long to know *Don John's* success.

D. Ant. He's engag'd upon a noble cause: if he succeeds, 'twill be a victory worth the owning.

D. Lop. Hah! whom have we here? a young man well habited, with a Lady too; they seem to be strangers.

D. Ant. A mischief comes into my head, that's worth the doing.

D. Lop. What's that, dear *Antonio?*

D. Ant. We are in a strange Countrey, and may want money: I would rob that young Fellow. We have not robb'd a good while; me-thinks 'tis a new wickedness to me.

D. Lop. Thou art in the right. I hate to commit the same dull sin over and over again, as if I were marri'd to it: variety makes all things pleasant.

D. Ant. But there's one thing we'll ne'r omit. When we have robb'd the Man, we'll ravish the Woman.

D. Lop. Agreed; let's to't, man. Come on, young Gentleman, we must see what riches you have about you.

Mar. O Villains! Thieves! Thieves! these are the inhumane Companions of that bloudy Monster.

Leon. Have pity on poor miserable Strangers.

D. Ant. Peace; we'll use you kindly, very kindly.

D. Lop. Do you carry that young Gentleman, bind him to a Tree, and bring the money, while I wait upon the Lady.

D. Ant. Will you play me no foul play in the mean time then? For we must cast Lots about the business you wot of.

D. Lop. No, upon my honour.

Mar. Honour, you Villain?

D. Ant. Come, young Gentleman, I'll tame you.

Mar. Help! help―――― [*Exit* Don Ant. *haling* Maria.

Leon. Have you no humanity in you? Take our money, but leave us liberty; be not so barb'rously cruel.

D. Ant. Come, I have made haste with him; now let us draw

Cuts,

Cuts who enjoys the Lady firſt.

Leon. O heav'n aſſiſt me! what do I hear? help! help!

Enter four or five Countrey Fellows, coming from work.

1. *Count. Fel.* What, two men a robbing of a Lady! Be gone, and let her alone, or we have ſower Cudgels ſhall waller your bones, I tell you that.

D. Ant. How now, Rogues?　　　　　 [*Fight off the Stage.*

Leon. Thanks to Heav'n. I fly! I fly! where ſhall I hide my ſelf?———　　　　　　　　　　　　　[*Exit.*

Enter Don John *and* Jacomo.

D. Joh. I ſhall conquer 'em both. Now, Sirra, what think you?

Jac. Why I think you manage your buſineſs as diſcreetly, and take as much pains to have your throat cut, as any man in *Spain.*

D. Joh. Your fear o'r-rules your ſenſe, mine is a life Monarchs might envy.———

Jac. 'Tis like to be a very ſhort one at this rate.

D. Joh. Away, Fool, 'tis dark, I muſt be gone; I ſhall ſcarce find the way home ———

Enter Leonora.

Leon. Heav'n guard me from theſe wicked Wretches. Help! help! they are here.

D. Joh. How now, Madam? what, afraid of a Man!

Leon. Don John, no, not of you; you are the man i'th' world I wou'd have met.

D. Joh. Leonora, you are the woman i'th' world I would have avoided. 'Sdeath! ſhe will ſpoil my new deſigns; but I have a trick for her. What miracle brought you hither?

Leon. Love, that works the greateſt miracles, made me follow you; and the ſame Storm drove me on this ſhoar, on which you were thrown, and thus far I've wander'd till I have found you.

D. Joh. This is the moſt unreaſonable unſatiable loving Lady, that ever was abus'd by man; ſhe has a kind of Spaniel love,

the

the worfe you ufe her, the more loving fhe is. Pox on her, I muft be rid of her.

Leon. I am very faint and weary, yet I was refolv'd not to reft till I had found you.

D. Joh. Your unweari'd love has o'rcome and convinc'd me, there is not fuch a Woman breathing.

Leon. This is a Sovereign Medicine for all my forrows, I now, methinks, am happier than ever: but I am faint and ill.

D. Joh. Here, Madam, I have an excellent Cordial, 'twill refrefh you; and I'll conduct you where you fhall never be unhappy more.

Leon. From that dear hand 'tis welcome ———
To your health.   [*Drinks.*

D. Joh. And to your own deftruction; you have drunk your laft.

Leon. What means my Love?

D. Joh. Y'have drunk the fubtleft poifon that Art e'r yet invented.

Jac. O murder! murder! what have you done?

D. Joh. Peace, Villain, leave your unfeafonable pity ——
You cannot live two minutes.

Leon. O ungrateful Tyrant! thou haft murder'd the onely Creature living that cou'd love thee. Heaven will revenge it, though to me 'tis kindnefs. Here all my forrows fhall for ever ceafe.

D. Joh. Why would you perfecute me with your love?

Leon. I could not help it. I came to preferve you, and am deftroy'd for't.

Jac. Oh horrid fact!

D. Joh. To preferve me! I wear my fafety by my fide.

Leon. Oh I faint! Guard your felf. There's a young Gentleman purfues your life. Have a Care ———
I came to tell you this, and thus I am rewarded.
Heav'n pardon you. Farewell. I can no more.   [*Dies.*

Jac. This object fure will ftrike your heart! Tygers would melt at this. Oh the Earth will open and fwallow you up, and me for company. There's no end of your murders ———

D. Joh. This is the firft time I ever knew compaffion.
Poor Fool, I pity her, but 'tis too late.——   Farewell

Farewell all fenfleft thoughts of a remorfe,
I would remove what e'r wou'd ftop my courfe.   [*Exeunt.*

ACT IV.

Enter Don John, Don Lopez, Don Antonio, Jacomo.

D. Joh. THis nights fuccefs exceeded all my hopes. I had ad-
mittance to their feveral Chambers, and I have
been contracted to both the Sifters, and this day refolve to marry 'em, and at feveral times enjoy them ; and, in my opinion, I
fhall have a brace of as pretty Wives, as any man in *Spain.*

D. Ant. Brave *Don John,* you are Mafter of your Art, not a
Woman in *Spain* can ftand before you.

D. Lop. We can but envy you, and at a diftance imitate ; But
both their Maids fhall to pot, I affure you.

Jac. How far will the Devil hurry you ?

D. Joh. 'Tis not the Devil, 'tis the Flefh, Fool.

Jac. Here will be fine cutting of throats. Poor *Jacomo,* muft
thou be cut off in the flower of thy Age ?

Enter Don Francifco.

D. Fran. Gentlemen, your Servant ; I hope you refted well
this night.

D. Lop. We thank you, Sir ; never better.

D. Ant. We never fhall requite this obligation.

Jac. I warrant you my Mafter will ; he's a very grateful civil
perfon indeed.

D. Joh. The favour is too great to be fuddenly requited ; but
I fhall ftudy to deferve it.

Jac. Good man, you will deferve it.

Enter two Bridegrooms.

D. Fran. Gentlemen, you are come, you are early.

1. Brid.

1. *Brideg.* This joyful occasion made us think it late.

2. *Brideg.* The expectation of so great a blessing as we this day hope to enjoy, would let us have but little rest last night.

1. *Brideg.* And the fruition will afford us less to night.

D. Joh. Poor Fools! you shall be bob'd. How it tickles my Spleen to think on't.

D. Fran. These are to be my Sons in Law.

D. Joh. And my Cuckolds before-hand.

D. Fran. Pray know 'em, Gentlemen; they are men of Honour.

D. Joh. I shall be glad to serve them; But first I'll serve their Ladies.   [*Aside.*

D. Fran. Come, Gentlemen, I'll now conduct you to my Daughters; and beg your pardon for a moment, I'll wait on you again.   [*Exit* Don Fran. *and Bridegrooms.*

D. Ant. These Fools will spoil your design.

D. Joh. No, poor Sots; I have persuaded the Ladies to feign sickness, and put off their marriage till to morrow morning, to gain time; in the mean while I have 'em safe, Boys.

D. Lop. But will not the Sisters betray you to one another?

D. Joh. No, I have wheedled each into a jealousie of the other, and each believes, that if the other knows it, she, in honour, will reveal it to the Father.

Jac. Sir, if you be so very weary of your life, why don't you make use of a convenient Beam? 'tis the easier way; so you may die without the filthy pother you keep about it.

D. Joh. Away, Coward; 'tis a sign I am not weary of my life, that I make so much use on't.

Jac. Oh *Jacomo*! thou art lost; 'tis pity a Fellow of thy neat spruce parts should be destroy'd.

Enter Don Francisco.

D. Fran. Come, Gentlemen, will you not refresh your selves with some cool Wines this morning?

D. Lop. We thank you, Sir, we have already.

Enter

Enter a Servant

Serv. Sir, here's a young Gentleman, a Stranger, defires to speak with you.

D. Fran. Admit him.

Enter Maria in Mor's habit.

Your humble Servant.

Mar. Sir, when I've told you what I come for, I doubt not but I shall deferve your thanks. I come to do you fervice.

D. Fran. You have 'em, Sir, already————

Mar. You have lodg'd within your houfe fome shipwrack'd men, who are greater Villains than the Earth e'r bore; I come to give you warning of 'em, and to beg your power to revenge fuch horrid actions, as heart could never yet conceive, or tongue could utter. Ha! they are thefe—— Revenge, revenge cruel, unnatural Rapes and Murders. They are Devils in the fhapes of men.

D. Fran. What fay you, Sir?

Jac. Now the fnare is faln upon me; me-thinks I feel cold Steel already in my body. Too well I know that face.

D. Joh. I know that face. Now, Impudence, affift me. What mad young man is that?

D. Fran. Thefe, by their habits and their meens, are Gentlemen, and feem to be men of Honour.

Mar. By thefe two, laft night, I was robb'd, and bound to a Tree, and there have been all night, and but this morning was reliev'd by Peafants———— I had a Lady with me, whom they faid they would ravifh, and this morning I faw her dead; they muft have murder'd her.

D. Fran. Heav'n! what do I hear?

Jac. Oh! I am noos'd already, I feel the knot, methinks, under my left ear.

D. Ant. The youth raves; we never faw his face, we never ftirr'd from the bounds of this houfe fince we came hither.

D. Lop. 'Sdeath, let me kill the Villain; fhall he thus affront men of our quality and honour? *D. Fran.*

D. Fran. Hold, confider I am a Magiftrate.

D. Joh. The Youth was robb'd, and with the fright has loft, his wits. Poor Fool! let him be bound in's bed.

D. Fran. Do not perfift in this, but have a care: Thefe injuries to men of Honour fhall not go unpunifhed.

Mar. Whither fhall injur'd Innocence fly for fuccour, if you fo foon can be corrupted? Monfter, I'll revenge my felf; have at thy heart.

D. Fran. What means the Youth? put up your Sword.

D. Ant. We told you, Sir, he was mad.

Mar. Oh impudent Villains! I ask your pardon, Sir: My griefs and injuries tranfport me fo, I fcarce can utter them. That Villain is *Don John,* who bafely murder'd the Governour of *Sevil* in his houfe, and then difhonour'd his fair Sifter.

D. Joh. Death and Hell! this injury is beyond all fufferance.

D. Joh. Hold, Sir, think in whofe houfe you are.

Jac. O Lord! what will this come to? Ah *Jacomo*! thy line of life is fhort.

Mar. This is the Villain, who kill'd the Lover of *Antonio's* Sifter, deflow'd her, and murder'd her Brother in his own houfe.

D. Joh. I'll have no longer patience.

D. Ant. Such a Villain fhould have his throat cut, though in a Church.

D. Lop. No man of honour will protect thofe, who offer fuch injuries.

D. Joh. Have at you, Villain.

D. Fran. Nay then; Within there: Ho! I will protect him, or perifh with him.

Enter two Bridegrooms.

1. *Brideg.* What's the matter?

D. Joh. This rafhnefs will fpoil my defign upon the Daughters; if I had perfected that, I would have own'd all this for half a Duccatoon ——— [*To* Ant. Lop.
I ask your pardon for my ill manners; I was provok'd too far: indeed the accufations are fo extravagant and odd, I rather

fhould

should have laugh'd at 'em. Let the young Fool have a vein open'd, he's stark staring mad.

D. Ant. A foolish Impostor. We ne'r saw *Sevil* till last night.

Mar. Oh Impudence!

Jac. No, not we; we never were there till yesterday. Pray, Sir, lay that young Fellow by the heels, for lying on us, men of Honour.

D. Fran. What is the matter, Friend, you tremble so?

D. Lop. 'Sdeath, the Dog's fear will betray us.

Jac. I tremble, Sir? no, no, Sir: I tremble —————— Though it would make any one tremble to hear one lie, as that young Gentleman does. Have you no conscience in you?

Mar. Heav'n can witness for me, I speak not false. *Octavio*, my dear *Octavio*, being dearest to me of all the world, I would in *Sevil* have reveng'd his murder; but the Villain there escap'd me: I follow'd him to Sea, and in the same Storm in which their Ship perish'd, I was thrown on shoar. Oh my *Octavio*! if this foul unnatural murther be not reveng'd, there is no Justice left among mankind. His Ghost, and all the rest whom he has barbarously murder'd, will interrupt your quiet; they'll haunt you in your sleep. Revenge, revenge!

2. Bride. This is wonderful.

D. Fran. There must be something in this; his passion cannot be counterfeited, nor your man's fear.

Jac. My fear? I scorn your words; I fear nothing under the Sun. I fear? Ha, ha, ha ————

D. Joh. Will you believe this one false Villain against three, who are Gentlemen, and men of honour?

Jac. Nay, against four, who are Gentlemen, and men of honour?

Mar. O Villain, that I had my Sword imbru'd in thy hearts bloud. Oh my dear *Octavio*! Do Justice, Sir, or Heav'n will punish you.

Enter Clara.

D. Fran. Gentlemen, he is too earnest, in his grief and anger, to be what you wou'd have him, an Impostor. My house has

been

been your Sanctuary, and I am oblig'd in honour not to act as a Magistrate, but your Host, no violence shall here be offer'd to you; but you must instantly leave this house, and if you would have safety, find it somewhere else. Be gone.

D. Joh. This is very well.

Mar. Oh! will you let 'em go unpunish'd? Whither shall I flie for vengeance?

D. Fran. Pray leave this place immediately.

Jac. Ah, good Sir, let's be gone —— Sir, your most humble Servant.

Clar. Oh, Sir, consider what you do; do not banish *Don John* from hence.

1. *Brideg.* Ha! what means she?

D. Fran. What say you?

Clar. Oh, Sir, he is my Husband, we were last night contracted.

D. Fran. Oh Heav'n! what do I hear?

1. *Brideg.* I am dishonour'd, abus'd. Villain, thou diest.

D. Joh. Villain, you lie; I will cut your throat first.

D. Fran. Hey, where are my people here.

Enter Servants and Flavia.

Flav. Oh, Sir, hold; if you banish *Don John*, I am lost for ever.

D. Fran. Oh Devil! what do I hear?

Flav. He is my Husband, Sir, we were last night contracted.

Clar. Your Husband! Heav'n! what's this?

2. *Brideg.* Hell and Damnation!

D. Fran. Oh! I have lost my senses.

Mar. Oh Monster! now am I to be believ'd?

Jac. Oh spare my life! I am innocent as I hope to live and breath.

D. Joh. Dog, you shall fight for your life, if you have it.

D. Franc. First, I'll revenge my self on these.

D. Joh. Hold, hold, they are both my Wives, and I will have them.

[*Runs at his Daughters, they run out.*
D. Franc.

D. Franc. Oh Devil! fall on————
Mar. Fall on, I will affift you.

[*They fight,* Maria *and* Don Francifco *are* kill'd, *the two Bridegrooms are hurt,* Jacomo *runs away.*

D. Joh. Now we've done their bufinefs.
Ah, cowardly Rogue! are not you a Son of a Whore?

Jac. Ay, Sir, what you pleafe: A man had better be a living Son of a Whore, than a dead *Hero,* by your favour.

D. Joh. I could find in my heart to kill the Rafcal; his fear, fome time or other, will undo us.

Jac. Hold, Sir; I went, Sir, to provide for your efcape. Let's take Horfes out of the Stable, and flie; abundance of Company are coming, expecting the Wedding, and we are irreparably loft if we take not this time. I think my fear will now preferve you.

D. Ant. I think he counfels well. Let's flie to a new place of pleafure.

D. Joh. But I fhall leave my bufinefs undone with the two Women.

D. Lop. 'Tis now fcarce feizible. Let's fly; you'll light on others as handfom, where we come next.

D. Joh. Well, difpofe of me as you pleafe; and yet it troubles me.

Jac. Hafte, hafte, or we fhall be apprehended.   [*Exeunt.*

Enter Clara *and* Flavia.

Flav. O that I ever liv'd to fee this day!
This fatall day! 'Twas our vile difobedience
Caus'd our poor Father's death, which Heav'n
Will revenge on us. So lewd a Villain
As *Don John* was never heard of yet.

Clar. That we fhould be fo credulous! Oh dreadful
Accident! Dear Father, what Expiation can
We make? our crime's too foul for
Tears to wafh away, and all our lives will
Be too fhort, to fpend in penitence for this
Our levity and difobedience. He was the

Reft

Best of Fathers, and of Men.

Flav. What will become of us, poor miserable Maids,
Lost in our Fortunes and our Reputations?
Our intended Husbands, if they recover of their
Wounds, will murder us; and 'tis but Justice:
Our lives too now cannot be worth the keeping.
The Devils in the shapes of men are fled.

Clar. Let us not waste our time in fruitless grief;
Let us employ some to pursue the murderers.
And for our selves, let's to the next Monastery,
And there spend all our weary life in penitence.

Flav. Let's fly to our last Sanctuary in this world,
And try, by a Religious life, to expiate this Crime:
There is no safety, or no hope but there.
Let's go, and bid a long farewell to all the
World; a thing too vain, and little worth our care.

Clar. Agreed; farewell to all the vanity on Earth,
Where wretched Mortals, toss'd 'twixt hope and fear,
Must of all fix'd and solid joy despair.   [*Exeunt.*

The Scene is a delightful Grove.

Enter two Shepherds and two Nimphs.

1. *Shep.* Come Nimphs and Shepherds, haste away
To th'happy Sports within these shady Groves,
In pleasant lives time slides away apace,
But with the wretched seems to creep too slow.

1. *Nimph.* Our happy leisure we employ in joys,
As innocent as they are pleasant. We,
Strangers to strife, and to tumultuous noise,
To baneful envy, and to wretched cares,
In rural pleasures spend our happy days,
And our soft nights in calm and quiet sleeps.

2. *Shep.* No rude Ambition interrupts our rest,
Nor base and guilty thoughts how to be great.

2. *Nimph.* In humble Cottages we have such contents,
As uncorrupted Nature does afford,

Which

Which the great, that surfeit under gilded Roofs,
And wanton in Down Beds, can never know.

  1. Shep. Nature is here not yet debauch'd by Art,
'Tis as it was in *Saturn*'s happy days:
Minds are not here by Luxury invaded;
A homely Plenty, with sharp Appetite,
Does lightsome health, and vigorous strength impart.

  1. Nimph. A chast-cold Spring does here refresh our thirst,
Which by no feavourish surfeit is increas'd;
Our food is such as Nature meant for Men,
Ere with the Vicious, Eating was an Art.

  2. Nimph. In noisie Cities riot is persu'd,
And lewd luxurious living softens men,
Effeminates Fools in Body and in Mind,
Weakens their Appetites, and decays their Nerves.

  2. Shep. With filthy steams from their excess of Meat,
And clowdy vapours rais'd from dangerous Wine;
Their heads are never clear or free to think,
They waste their lives in a continual mist.

  1. Shep. Some subtil and ill men chuse Temperance,
Not as a Vertue, but a Bawd to Vice,
And vigilantly wait to ruine those,
Whom Luxury and Ease have lull'd asleep.

  2. Shep. Yes, in the clamorous Courts of tedious Law,
Where what is meant for a relief's a gievance;
Or in Kings Palaces, where Cunning strives,
Not to advance King's Interests, but its own.

  1. Nimph. There they in a continual hurry live,
And seldom can, for all their subtile Arts,
Lay their foundations sure; but some
Are undermin'd, others blown down by storms.

  2. Nimph. Their subtilty is but a common Road
Of flattering great men, and oppressing little,
Smiling on all they meet, and loving none.

  1. Shep. In populous Cities, life is all a storm;
But we enjoy a sweet perpetual calm:
Here our own Flocks we keep, and here
I and my *Phillis* can embrace unenvi'd.

2. Shep.

2. *Shep.* And I and *Celia* without jealousie.
But hark, the Pipes begin; now for our sports.
[*A Symphony of Rustick Musick.*

N Imphs and Shepherds come away,
In these Groves let's sport and play;
Where each day is a Holy-day,
Sacred to Ease and happy Love.
To Dancing, Musick, Poetry:
Your Flocks may now securely rove.
Whilst you express your jollity.

Enter Shepherds and Shepherdesses, singing in *Chorus*

We come, we come, no joy like this.
Now let us sing, rejoyce, and kiss.
The Great can never know such bliss
1. *As this.*
2. *As this.*
3. *As this.*
All. *As this.*
The Great can never know such bliss

1. *All th' Inhabitants o'th' Wood,*
Now celebrate the Spring,
That gives fresh vigour to the bloud
Of every living thing.
Chor. *The Birds have been singing and billing before us,*
And all the sweet Choristers joyn in the Chorus.

2. *The Nightingales with jugging throats,*
Warble out their pretty Notes,
So sweet, so sweet, so sweet:
And thus our Loves and Pleasures greet.
Chor. *Then let our Pipes sound, let us dance, let us sing,*
Till the murmuring Groves with loud Eccho's shall ring.
[*Dance begins*

K   *How*

4. *How happy are we,*
   From all jealousie free;
No dangers or cares can annoy us :
   We toy and we kiss,
   And Love's our chief bliss ;
A pleasure that never can cloy us.
Chor. *Our days we consume in uncmix'd delights,*
   And in love and soft rest our happy long nights.

4. *Each Nimph does impart*
   Her love without Art,
To her Swain, who thinks that his chief Treasure.
   No envy is fear'd,
   No sighs are e'r heard,
But those which are caus'd by our pleasure.
Chor. *When we feel the bless'd Raptures of innocent Love,*
   No joys exceed ours but the pleasures above.

General Chorus.
In these delightful fragrant Groves,
Let's celebrate our happy Loves.
Let's pipe, and dance, and laugh, and sing ;
Thus every happy living thing,
Revels in the cheerful Spring.

[Dance continues.

Enter Don John, Don Lopez, Don Antonio, Jacomo.

D. *Joh.* So, thus far we are safe, we have almost kill'd our Horses with riding cross out of all Roads.

Jac. Nay, you have had as little mercy on them, as if they had been Men or Women : But yet we are not safe, let us fly farther.

D. *Joh.* The house I lighted at was mine during my life, which I sold to that fellow ; he, since he holds by that tenure, will carefully conceal us.

Jac. Tis a Tenure I will not give him two moneths purchase for.

D. *Joh.* Besides, our Swords are us'd to conquest.

A m

D. Ant. At worſt, there is a Church hard by; we'll put it to its proper uſe, take refuge in't.

D. Lop. Look here, here are Shepherds, and young pretty Wenches; ſhall we be idle, *Don ?*

D. Ant. By no means; 'tis a long time, methinks, ſince we were vicious.

D. Joh. We'll ſerve 'em as the *Romans* did the *Sabines,* we'll rob 'em of their Women; onely we'll return the Punks again, when we have us'd them.

Jac. For Heav'ns ſake hold.

D Joh. Sirra, no more; do as we do, raviſh, Raſcal, or, by my Sword, I'll cut thee into ſo many pieces, it ſhall poſe an Arithmetician to ſum up the fractions of thy body.

Jac. I raviſh! Oh, good Sir! my courage lies not that way; alas, I, I am almoſt famiſh'd, I have not eat to day.

D Joh. Sirra, by Heaven do as I bid thee, or thou ſhalt never eat again. Shall I keep a Raſcal for a Cypher?

Jac. Oh! what will become of me? I muſt do it.

D. Joh. Come on, Rogue, fall on.

D. Ant. Which are you for?

D. Joh. 'Tis all one, I am not in Love but in Luſt, and to ſuch a one a Belly-full's a Belly-full, and there's an end on't.

1. Shepherdeſs. What means this violence?

2. Shepherdeſs. Oh! Heav'n protect us.

Jac. Well, I muſt have one too; if I be hang'd, I had as good be hang'd for ſomething.

[*Every one runs off with a Woman.*

D. Lop. Rogues, come not on; we'll be in your guts.

All Shepherdeſs. Help, help.   [*They cry out.*

1. Shep. What Devils are theſe ?   [*Exeunt.*

[*Three or four Shepherds return with* Jacomo.

1. Shep. Here's one Rogue. Have we caught you, Sir? we'll cool your courage.

Jac. Am I taken priſoner? I ſhall be kept as an honourable Hoſtage, at leaſt ———

2. Shep. Where are theſe Villains, theſe Raviſhers?

Jac. Why you need not keep ſuch a ſtir, Gentlemen, you will

K 2   have

have all your Women again, and no harm done. Let me go, I'll fetch 'em to you.

1. Shep. No, you libidinous Swine; we'll revenge the Rapes on you.

Jac. Good kind civil people pass this by: 'Tis true, my Master's a very *Tarquin*; but I ne'r attempted to ravish before.

2. Shep. I'll secure you from ever doing of it again. Where's your Knife?

Jac. Heav'n! what do you mean? Oh spare me! I am unprepar'd; let me be confest.

1. Shep. We will not kill you, we'll but geld you: Are you so hor, Sir?

Jac. Oh bloudy Villains! have a care, 'tis not a season for that, the Sign's in *Scorpio.*

2. Shep. Down with him————

Jac. O help, help! murder, murder! Have a care what you do, I am the last of all my Race———— Will you destroy a whole Stock, and take away my Representers of my Family?——

1. Shep. There shall be no more of the Breed of you

Jac. I am of an antient Family; will you cut off all hopes of a Son and Heir? Help! help! Master, *Don John?* Oh! Oh! Oh!

Enter Don John, Don Lopez, Don Antonio.

D. Joh. How now, Rogues? do you abuse my Man?

Jac. O Sir, this is the first good thing you ever did: if you had not come just in the Nick, I had lost my Manhood.

D. Ant. 'Tis no matter for the use you make on't.

D. Lop. But come, let's now to Supper.

Jac. Come on, I am almost starv'd.   [*Exeunt.*

Shepherds return.

1. Shep. Let's not complain, but Dog the Rogues, and when we have Hous'd 'em, we will to the next Magistrate, and beg his pow'r to apprehend 'em.   [*Exeunt.*

Scene

The Scene changes to a Church, with the Statue of *Don Pedro* on Horseback in it.

D. Joh. Let's in, and see this Church.

Jac. Is this a time to see Churches? But let me see whose Statue's this? Oh Heav'n! this is *Don Pedro's,* whom you murder'd at *Sevil.*

D. Joh. Say you so? Read the Inscription.

Jac. Here lies Don Pedro, *Governour of* Sevil, *barbarously murder'd by that impious Villain,* Don John, *'gainst whom his innocent blood cries still for vengeance.*

D. Joh. Let it cry on. Art thou there i'faith? · Yes, I kill'd thee, and wou'd do't again upon the same occasion. *Jacomo* —— invite him to Supper.

Jac. What, a Statue! invite a Statue to Supper? Ha, ha —— can Marble eat?

D. Joh. I say, Rascal, tell him I would have him Sup with me.

Jac. Ha, ha, ha! who the Devil put this whimsey into your head? Ha, ha, ha! invite a Statue to Supper?

D. Joh. I shall spoil your mirth, Sirra; I will have it done.

Jac. Why, 'tis impossible; wou'd you have me such a Coxcomb, invite Marble to eat? Ha, ha, ha.

> [*He goes several times towards the Statue, and returns laughing.*

Good Mr. Statue, if it shall please your Worship, my Master desires you to make Collation with him presently ————

> [*The Statue nods his head,* Jacomo *falls down and roars.*

Oh I am dead! Oh, Oh, Oh.

D. Joh. The Statue nods its head; 'tis odd ————

D. Ant. 'Tis wonderful.

D. Lop. I am amaz'd.

Jac. Oh I cannot stir! Help, help.

D. Joh. Well, Governour, come, take part of a Collation with me, 'tis by this time ready; make haste, 'tis I invite you.

> [*Statue nods again.*

Say you so? come on, let's set all things in order quickly.

Jac. Oh fly, fly.

D. Ant.

D. Ant. This is prodigious.

[*Exeunt* Don John, Don Lopez, Don Antonio, Jacomo.

The Scene is a Dining Room, a Table spread, Servants setting on Meat and Wine.

D. Joh. Come, our meat is ready, let's sit. Pox on this foolish Statue, it puzles me to know the reason on't. Sirra, I'll give you leave to sit.

D. Ant. Let's eat, ne'r think on't.

Jac. Ay, come, let's eat; I am too hungry now to think on the fright———— [*Jacomo eats greedily.*

D. Joh. This is excellent Meat. How the Rogue eats. You'll choak your self.

Jac. I warrant you, look to your self.

D. Ant. Why, *Jacomo*, is the Devil in you?

Jac. No, no; if he be, 'tis a hungry Devil.

D. Lop. Will you not drink?

Jac. I'll lay a good foundation first.

D. Joh. The Rascal eats like a Canibal.

Jac. Ay, 'tis no matter for that.

D. Joh. Some Wine, Sirra.

Jac. There, Sir, take it; I am in haste.

D. Ant. 'Sdeath, the Fool will be strangl'd.

Jac. The Fool knows what he does.

D. Joh. Here's to *Don Pedro's* Ghost, he should have been welcome.

Jac. O name him not.

D. Lop. The Rascal is afraid of you after death.

Jac. Oh! Oh! some Wine, give me some Wine.

[*Almost choak'd.*

D. Ant. Take it.

Jac. So, now 'tis down.

D. Ant. Are you not satisfi'd yet?

Jac. Peace, peace; I have but just begun.

[*One knocks hard at the door.*

Who's there? come in, I am very busie.

D. Joh.

D. Joh. Rise, and do your duty.

Jac. But one morsel more, I come.　　　[*Knocks again.*

What a pox, are you mad?　　　　　　　[*Opens the door.*

Enter Ghost.

Oh! the Devil, the Devil.

D. Joh. Hah! it is the Ghost, let's rise and receive him.

D. Ant. I am amaz'd.

D. Lop. Not frighted are you?

D. Ant. I scorn the thoughts of fear.

　　　　　　　　　　　　　　[*They salute the Ghost.*

D. Joh. Come, Governour, you are welcome, sit there; if we
had thought you would have come, we wou'd have staid for
you. But come on, Sirra, give me some Wine.　　[*The Ghost sits.*

Jac. Oh! I am dead; what shall I do? I dare not come near
you.

D, Joh. Come, Rascal, or I'll cut your throat.

　　　　　　　　　　[*Fills Wine, his hand trembles.*

Jac. I come, I come. Oh! Oh!

D. Joh. Why do you tremble, Rascal? hold it steadily ——

Jac. Oh! I cannot.

　　　　　　　[*Jacomo snatches meat from the Table,*
　　　　　　　　　　　　and runs aside.

D. Joh. Here, Governour, your health. Friends, put it about.
Here's excellent meat; taste of this Ragoust. If you had had a
body of flesh, I would have given you *cher entire* —————— but
the Women care not for Marble. Come, I'll help you. Come,
eat and let old quarrels be forgotten.

Ghost. I come not here to take repast with you;
Heaven has permitted me to animate
This Marble body and I come to warn
You of that vengeance is in store for you,
If you amend not your pernicious lives.

Jac. Oh Heav'n!

D. Ant. What, are you come to preach to us?

D. Lop. Keep your Harangues for Fools that will believe 'em.

D. Joh. We are too much confirm'd. Pox o' this dry discourse,

give me some Wine. Come, here's to your Miſtris; you had
one when you were living: not forgetting your ſweet Siſter.
Sirra, more Wine.

Jac. Ay, Sir——— Good Sir, do not provoke the *Ghoſt*; his
Marble fiſts may fly about your ears, and knock your brains
out.

D. Joh. Peace, Fool.

Ghoſt. Tremble, you impious Wretches, and repent ;
Behold, the pow'rs of Hell wait for you——— [*Devils riſe.*

Jac. Oh! I will ſteal from hence. Oh the Devil !

D. Joh. Sirra, ſtir not; by Heav'n I'll uſe thee worſe than
Devils can do. Come near, Coward.

Jac. O I dare not ſtir; what will become of me ?

D. Joh. Come, Sirra, eat.

Jac. O, Sir, my appetite is ſatisfied.

D. Joh. Drink, Dog, the *Ghoſt's* health: Rogue, do't, or I'll
run my Sword down your throat.

Jac. Oh! Oh! Here, Mr. *Statue,* your health.

D. Joh. Now, Raſcal, ſing to entertain him.

Jac. Sing, quoth he ! Oh ! I have loſt my voice; I cannot be
merry in ſuch company. Sing———

D. Ant. Who are theſe with ugly ſhapes ?

D. Lop. Their manner of appearing is ſomething ſtrange.

Ghoſt. They're Devils, that wait for ſuch hard impious
Men. They're Heavens Inſtruments of eternal vengeance.

D. Joh. Are they ſome of your Retinue ? Devils, ſay you ? I
am ſorry I have no Burnt Brandey to treat 'em with, that's Drink
fit for Devils——— Hah ! they vaniſh. [*They ſink.*

Ghoſt. Cannot the fear of Hell's eternal tortures,
Change the horrid courſe of your abandon'd lives ?
Think on thoſe Fires, thoſe everlaſting Fires,
That ſhall without conſuming burn you ever.

D. Joh. Dreams, dreams, too ſlight to loſe my pleaſure for.
In ſpight of all you ſay I will go on,
Till I have ſurfeited on all delights.
Youth is a Fruit that can but once be gather'd,
And I'll enjoy it to the full.

D. Ant.

D. Ant. Let's push it on; Nature chalks out the way that we should follow.

D. Lop. 'Tis her fault, if we do what we should not. Let's on, here's a Brimmer to our Leader's health.

Jac. What hellish Fiends are these?

D. Joh. Let me tell you, 'tis something ill bred to rail at your Host, that treats you civilly. You have not yet forgot your quarrel to me.

Ghost. 'Tis for your good; by me Heaven warns you of its wrath, and gives you a longer time for your repentance. I invite you this night to a repast of mine.

D. Joh. Where?

Ghost. At my Tomb.

D. Ant. What time?

Ghost. At dead of night.

D. Joh. We'll come.

Ghost. Fail not.

D. Lop. I warrant you.

Ghost. Farewell, and think upon your lost condition.

D. Joh. Farewell, Governour; I'll see what Treat you'll give us.

D. Ant. } And I.
D. Lop. }

Jac. That will not I. Pox on him, I have had enough of his company, I shall not recover it this week. If I eat with such an Host, I'll be hang'd.

D. Joh. If you do not, by Heaven you shall be hang'd.

Jac. Whither will your lewdness carry me? I do not care for having a Ghost for my Landlord. Will not these Miracles do good upon you?

D. Joh. There's nothing happens but by Natural Causes, Which in unusual things Fools cannot find, And then they stile 'em Miracles. But no Accident Can alter me from what I am by Nature. Were there———— Legions of Ghosts and Devils in my way, One moment in my course of pleasure I'd not stay.

[*Exeunt omnes*

L

ACT

ACT V.

Enter Jacomo, *with Back, Breaft, and Head-piece.*

Jac. WEll, this damn'd Mafter of mine will not part with me; and we muft fight five or fix times a day, one day with another, that's certain : Therefore thou art wife, honeft *Jacomo*, to arm thy felf, I take it. Sa, fa, fa ——— Methinks I am very valiant on the fudden. Sa, fa, fa. Hah! there I have you. Paph—— Have at you. Hah—— there I have you through : that was a fine thruft in tierce. Hah —— Death! what noife is that ?

Enter Don John.

D. Joh. How now, Sirra, what are you doing ?

Jac. Nothing, but practifing to run people through the bodies, that's all ; for I know fome body's throat muft be cut before midnight.

D. Joh. In Armour too ! why, that cannot help you, you are fuch a cowardly Fool ; fear will betray you fafter within, than that can defend you without———

Jac. I fear no body breathing, I ; nothing can terrifie me but the Devillifh Ghoft. Ha ! who's that coming? Oh Heaven !

[*Leaps back.*

D. Joh. Is this your courage ? you are preparing for flight before an Enemy appears.

Jac. No, no, Sir, not I ; I onely leapt back to put my felf upon my guard —— Fa, la, la ———

Enter Don Lopez *and* Don Antonio.

D. Joh. Whom have we here ?

Jac. Oh where ! where ! who are they ?

D. Joh. Oh my Friends! where have you been?

D. Ant.

D. Ant We went to view the stately Nunnery hard by, and have been chatting with the poor sanctifi'd Fools, till it's dark; we have been chaffering for Nuns-flesh.

D. Lop. There I made such a discovery, if you do not assist me, I am ruin'd for ever. *Don Bernardo's* Sister, whom I fell in love with in *Sevil*, is this day plac'd there for probation; and if you cannot advise me to some way or other of getting her out, for some present occasion I have for her, I am a lost man, that's certain.

D. Ant. The business is difficult, and we resolve to manage it in council.

Jac. Now will they bring me into some wicked occasion or other of shewing my prowess: a pox on 'em.

D. Joh. Have you so long followed my fortunes, to boggle at difficulty upon so honourable an occasion; besides, here is no difficulty.

D. Lop. No? the Walls are so high, and the Nunnery so strongly fortifi'd, 'twill be impossible to do it by force; we must find some stratagem.

D. Joh. The stratagem is soon found out ——

D. Ant. As how, *Don John?*

D. Joh. Why, I will set fire on the Nunnery; fire the Hive, and the Drones must out, or be burnt within: then may you, with ease, under pretence of succour, take whom you will.

D. Lop. 'Tis a gallant design.

D. Ant. I long to be about it. Well, *Don*, thou art the bravest Fellow breathing.

Jac. Gentlemen, pray what became of that brave Fellow, that fir'd the Temple at *Ephesus?* was he not hang'd, Gentlemen, hum ——

D. Ant. We are his Rivals, Fool; and who would not suffer for so brave an action?

D. Joh. He's a Scoundrel and a Poultroon, that would not have his Death for his Fame.

D. Lop. That he is, a damn'd Son of a Whore, and not fit to drink with.

Jac. 'Tis a rare thing to be a Martyr for the Devil; But what good will infamy do you, when you are dead? when Ho-

nour

nour is nothing but a vapour to you, while you are living. For my part I'd not be hang'd to be *Alexander the Great*. ·

D. Ant. What a phlegmatick dull Rascal is that, who has no Ambition in him.

Jac. Ambition! what, to be hang'd? besides, what's the intrinsick value of Honour when a man is under ground? Let 'em but call me honest *Jacomo*, as I am, while I live, and let 'em call me, when I am dead, *Don John* if they will.

D. Joh. Villain, dare you profane my name?

Jac. Hold, Sir, think what you do; you cannot hurt me, my Arms are Pistol-proof.

Enter a Servant.

Serv. I come to give you notice of an approaching danger: You must fly; an Officer with some Shepherds have found you were at our house, and are come to apprehend you, for some outrage you have committed; I came to give you notice, knowing our Family has a great respect for you.

D. Joh. Yes, I know your Family has a great respect for me, for I have lain with every one in it, but thee and thy Master.

Jac. Why look you now, I thought what 'twou'd come to: Fly, Sir, fly; the darkness of the night will help us. Come, I'll lead the way.

D. Joh. Stay, Sirra, you shall have one occasion more of showing your valour.

D. Ant. Did ever any Knight Errant fly, that was so well appointed?

D. Lop. No; you shall stay, and get Honour, *Jacomo*.

Jac. Pox of Honour, I am content with the Stock I have already.

D. Joh. You are easily satisfied. But now let's fire the Nunnery.

D. Ant. Come on.

D. Lop. I long to be at it.

Jac. O *Jacomo*! thy life is not worth a Piece of Eight. 'Tis in vain to disswade 'em, Sir; I will never trouble you with another

other requeſt, if you'll be gracioußy pleas'd to leave me out of this adventure.

D. Joh. Well, you have your deſire.

Jac. A thouſand thanks; and when I ſee you again, I will be humbly content with a Halter.

D. Joh. But, do you hear, Fool? ſtand Centinel here; and if any thing happens extraordinary, give us notice of it.

Jac. O, good Sir! what do you mean? that's as bad as going with you.

D. Joh. Let me find you here when I come again, or you are a dead man———

[*Exeunt* Don John, Don Lopez, Don Antonio.

Jac. I am ſure I am a dead man, if you find me here: But would my Armour were off now, that I might run the lighter. Night aſſiſt me. Heaven! what noiſe is that? to be left alone in the dark, and fear Ghoſts and Devils, is very horrible. But Oh! who are theſe?

Enter Officer, Guards, and Shepherds.

1. *Shep.* We are thus far right; the Raviſhers went this way.

2. *Shep.* For Heavens ſake take 'em dead or alive; ſuch deſperate Villains ne'r were ſeen.

Jac. So; if I be catch'd, I ſhall be hang'd; if not, I ſhall be kill'd. 'Tis very fine. Theſe are the Shepherds. I'll hide my ſelf.

[*He ſtands up cloſe againſt the Wall.*

1. *Shep.* If we catch the Rogues, we will broil 'em alive; no death can be painful enough for ſuch Wretches.

Jac. O bloudy minded men———

2. *Shep.* O impious vile Wretches! that we had you in our clutches! Open your Dark Lantern, and let's ſearch for 'em.

Jac. What will become of me? my Armour will not do now.

1. *Shep.* Thus far we hunted them upon a good ſcent: but now we are at a fault.

Jac. Let me ſee; I have one trick left, I have a Diſguiſe will fright the Devil.

2. *Shep.* They muſt be hereabouts.

Jac.

Jac. I'll in amongst them, and certainly this will fright 'em.

1. *Shep.* Oh Heav'n! what horrid Object's this?

Jac. The Devil.

2. *Shep.* Oh fly, fly! the Devil, the Devil! fly ———

[Exeunt Shepherds frighted.

Jac. Farewell, good Gentlemen. This is the first time my face e'r did me good. But I'll not stay I take it; Yet whether shall I fly? Oh! what noise is that? I am in the dark, in a strange place too; what will follow? There lie. Oh! my Arms. Hah! Who's there? Let me go this way ——— Oh the Ghost! the Ghost! Gad forgive me, 'twas nothing but my fear———

[A noise within, Fire, fire, the Nunnery's on fire.

Oh vile Wretches! they have done the deed. There is no flying; now the place will be full of people, and wicked Lights, that will discover me, if I fly.

Within. Fire, fire, fire; the Nunnery's on fire; help, help——

[Several people cross the Stage, crying Fire.

Jac. What shall I do? there's no way but one, I'll go with the Crowd. Fire! Fire —— Murder! help! help! fire! fire---

[More people cross the Stage, he runs with them.

Enter Don John, Don Antonio, Don Lopez, *four Nuns.*

D. Joh. Fear not, Ladies, we'll protect you.

1. *Nun.* Our Sex and Habits will protect us.

D. Lop. Not enough, we will protect you better.

1. *Nun.* Pray leave us, we must not consort with men.

D. Ant. What would you run into the fire to avoid Mankind? you are zealous Ladies indeed.

D. Joh. Come, Ladies, walk with us; we'll put you in a place of safety.

1. *Nun.* We'll go no further, we are safe enough; be gone, and help to quench the fire.

D. Joh. We have another fire to quench; come along with us.

D. Lop. Ay, come, you must go.

D. Ant.

D. Ant. Come along, we know what's good for you; you must go with us.

1. *Nun* Heaven! what violence is this? what impious men are these? Help! help!　　　　　　　　　　[*All cry Help.*

Enter Flavia *and* Clara, *Probationers.*

Flav. Here are the bloudy Villains, the causes of our misery.

Clar. Inhumane Butchers! now we'll have your lives.

D. Joh. Hah! here are a brace of my Wives. If you have a mind to this Fool, take her betwixt you; for my part, I'll have my own. Come, Wives, along with me; we must consummate, my Spouses, we must consummate.

Clar. What Monsters are these?

All Nuns. Help! help!

D. Ant. 'Sdeath! these foolish Women are their own Enemies.

D. Lop. Here are so many people, if they cry out more, they'll interrupt us in our brave design.

D. Joh. I warrant you; when they cry out, let us out-noise 'em. Come, Women, you must go along with us.

1. *Nun.* Heaven! what shall we do? Help! help!

D. Joh. Help! help! Fire! fire! fire!

D. Lop. }
D. Ant. } Help! help!

[*They hale the Women by the hands, who still cry out, and they with them.*

Enter several people, crying out Fire, Jacomo *in the rear.*

Jac. Fire! fire! fire! Help! help! 'Sdeath! here's my Master,

D. Joh. Sirra, come along with me, I have use of you.

Jac. I am caught.

D. Joh. Here, Sirra, take one of my Wives, and force her after me. Do you refuse, Villain?

Enter Shepherds, with Officer and Guards.

Nuns. Help! help! good people help! rescue us from these Villains.

1. *Shep.* Who are you, committing violence on Women?

2. *Shep.* Heavens! they are the Villains we seek for.

Jac. Where is my Armour now? Oh my Armour.

Officer. Fall on.

> [*They fight, Women fly,* Jacomo *falls down as kill'd, two Shepherds and the Officer are kill'd.*

D. Joh. Say you so, Rogues?

D. Lop. So, the Field's our own.

D. Joh. But a pox on't, we have bought a Victory too dear, we have lost the Women.

D. Ant. We'll find 'em again. But poor *Jacomo's* kill'd.

Jac. That's a lie.   [*Aside.*

D. Lop. 'Faith, let's carry off our dead.

D. Joh. Agreed; we'll bury him in the Church, while the Ghost treats us, we'll treat the Worms with the body of a Rascal.

Jac. Not yet a while.   [*Aside.*

D. Lop. Come, let's take away the Fool.

Jac. No, the Fool can take up himself. 'Sdeath! you resolve not to let me alone dead or alive——
Here are more Murders. Oh!

D. Lop. Oh counterfeiting Rascal! are you alive?

> [*The Clock strikes Twelve.*

D. Ant. The Clock strikes Twelve.

D. Joh. 'Slife, our times come, we must to the Tomb: I would not break my word with the Ghost for a thousand Doubloons——

Jac. Nor I keep it for ten times the Money.

D. Joh. But you shall keep your word, Sir.

Jac. Sir, I am resolv'd to fast to night, 'tis a Vigil: Besides, I care not for eating in such base company.

Within. Follow, follow, follow——

D. Lop. D' hear that noise? the remaining Rogues have rais'd the Mobile, and are coming upon us.

Jac. Oh! let's flie—— flie—— what will become of me?

D. Ant. Let's to the Church, and give the Rogues the Go-by.

D. Joh. Come on, since 'tis my time, and I have promis'd the Governour, I'll go—— You had best stay, Sirra, and be taken.

Jac. No : now I must go to the Church whether I will or no. Away, away, flie !

Enter two Shepherds, with a great Rabble.

Here they went; follow, follow ——   [*Exeunt omnes.*

The Scene the Church, the Statue of *Don Pedro* on Horseback ; on each side of the Church, *Don John's* Ghost, *Maria's*, *Don Francisco's*, *Leonora's*, *Flora's*, *Maria's* Brothers, and others, with Torches in their hands.

Enter Don John, Don Antonio, Don Lopez, Jacomo.

Jac. Good Sir, let's go no farther ; look what horrid Attendants are here. This wicked Ghost has no good meaning in him.

D. Joh. He resolves to treat us in State ; I think he has robb'd all the Graves hereabouts of their Dead, to wait upon us.

D. Ant. I see no Entertainment prepar'd.

D. Lop. He has had the manners to light off his Horse, and entertain us.

D. Joh. He would not sure be so ill bred, to make us wait on him on foot.

Jac. Pox on his breeding, I shall die with fear ; I had as good have been taken and hang'd. What horror seizes me !

D. Joh. Well, Governour, you see we are as good as our words.

D. Ant. Where's your Collation?

D. Lop. Bid some of your Attendants give us some Wine.

[*Ghost descends.*

M   *Stat.*

Stat. Have you not yet thought on your loft condition?
Here are the Ghofts of fome whom you have murder'd,
That cry for vengeance on you————

Fathers Ghoft. Repent, repent of all your horrid crimes:
Monfters, repent, or Hell will fwallow you.

D. Joh. That's my Old man's voice. D'hear, Old Gentleman
you talk idly.

Ju. I do repent, O fpare me. I do repent of all my fins, but
efpecially of following this wicked Wretch.   [*Kneel*

D. Ant. Away, Fool   [Ant. *kicks him*

D. Fran. Ghoft. My bloud cries out upon thee, barbarous
Wretch.

D. Joh. That's my Hoft *Francifco*, 'faith thou wert a good honeft Blockhead, that's the truth on't————

Flora's Ghoft. Thou fhalt not efcape vengeance for all thy
crimes.

D. Joh. What Fool's that, I am not acquainted with her.

Leon. Ghoft. In time lay hold on mercy, and repent.

D. Joh. That was *Leonora*, a good natur'd filly Wench, fomething too loving, that was all her fault.

Mar. Villain, this is the laft moment of thy life,
And thou in flames eternally fhalt howl.

D. Joh. Thou li'ft. This is the young hot-headed Fool we
kill'd at *Francifco's*. Pox on him, he difappointed me in my defign upon the Daughters. Would thou wert alive again, that I
might kill thee once more.

D. Lop. No more of this old foolifh ftuff; give us fome Wine
to begin with.

D. Ant. Ay, give us fome Wine, Governour.

D. Joh. What, do you think to treat us thus? I offer'd you
better entertainment. Prethee trouble us no more, but bid
fome of your Attendants give us fome Wine; I'll drink to you
and all the good Company.

Stat. Give em the Liquor they have moft delighted in.
      [*Two of the Ghofts go out, and bring
        four Glaffes full of bloud, then give 'em to
        D. John, D. Ant. D. Lop.*

D. Lop. This is fomething.

D. J.

D. Joh. This is civil.

D. Lop. I hope a good defert will follow.

        [*Ghoft offers a Glafs to* Jacomo,
          who runs round D. John, D. Ant.
           D. Lop. *roaring.*

Jac. Are you ftark diftracted? will you drink of that Liquor?
Oh! Oh! what d'you mean? Good fweet Ghoft forbear your
civility; Oh I am not dry, I thank you ————

D. Joh. Give it me. Here, take it, Sirra.

Jac. By no means, Sir, I never drink between meals. Oh Sir—

D. Joh. Take it, Rafcal.

Jac. Oh Heav'ns!

D. Joh. Now, Governour, your Health; 'tis the reddeft drink
I ever faw.

D. Lop. Hah! pah! 'tis bloud.

D. Ant. Pah! it is ————

Jac. Oh! I'll have none of it.

           [*They throw the Glaſſes down.*

D. Joh. 'Sdeath, do you mean to affront us?

Stat. 'Tis fit for fuch bloud-thirfty Wretches.

D. Joh. Do you upbraid me with my killing of you; I did it,
and would do it again: I'd fight with all your Family one by
one; and cut off root and branch to enjoy your Sifter. But will
you treat us yet no otherwife?

Stat. Yes, I will, ye impious Wretches.   [*A Flouriſh.*

D. Lop. What's here? Mufick to treat us with?

D. Ant. There is fome pleafure in this.

           Song of Devils.

1. Dev. *PRepare, prepare, new Guefts draw near,*
           And on the brink of Hell appear.
2. Dev. *Kindle freſh flames of Sulphur there.*
           Aſſemble all ye Fiends,
           Wait for the dreadful ends
           Of impious men, who far excel
           All th' Inhabitants of Hell.

Chor. of — *Let 'em come, let 'em come,*
Devils. { *To an eternal dreadful doom,*
            Let 'em come, let 'em come.

3. Dev. *In mischiefs they have all the damn'd out done;*
      Here they shall weep, and shall unpiti'd groan,
      Here they shall howl, and make eternal moan.

1. Dev. *By Bloud and Lust they have deserv'd so well,*
      That they shall feel the hottest flames of Hell.

2. Dev. *In vain they shall here their past mischiefs bewail,*
      In exquisite torments that never shall fail.

3. Dev.   *Eternal darkness they shall find,*
        And them eternall Chains shall bind
        To infinite pain of sense and mind.

Chorus — *Let 'em come, let 'em come,*
of all. { *To an eternal dreadful doom*
           Let 'em come, let 'em come.

Stat. Will you not relent, and feel remorse?

D. Joh. Cou'dst thou bestow another heart on me, I might; but with this heart I have, I cannot.

D. Lop. These things are prodigious.

D. Ant. I have a kind of grudging to relent, but something holds me back.

D. Lop. If we could, 'tis now too late; I will not.

D. Ant. We defie thee.

Stat. Perish, ye impious Wretches, go and find
The punishments laid up in store for you.
                [*It Thunders,* Don Lopez *and* Don
                    Antonio *are swallow'd up.*
Behold their dreadful Fates, and know, that thy last moment's come.

D. Joh. Think not to fright me, foolish Ghost; I ll break your Marble body in pieces, and pull down your Horse.

Jac. If fear has left me my strength, I'll steal away.   [*Exit.*

D. Joh. These things I see with wonder, but no fear.

                                    Were

Were all the Elements to be confounded,
And shuffl'd all into their former Chaos;
Were Seas of *Sulphur* flaming round about me,
And all Mankind roaring within those fires,
I could not fear or feel the least remorse.
To the last instant I would dare thy power.
Here I stand firm, and all thy threats contemn;
Thy Murderer stands here, now do thy worst.

> [*It Thunders and Lightens*, *Devils descend
> and sink with* Don John, *who is cover'd
> with a Clowd of fire as he sinks.*

Stat. Thus perish all,
Those men, who by their words and actions dare,
Against the will and power of Heaven declare.

> [*Scene shuts.*

E P I-

EPILOGUE,

Spoken by *Jacomo*.

THrough all the Perils of the Play I've run,
But know not how your fury I may shun;
I'm in new dangers now to be undone ——
I had but one fierce Master there,
But I have many cruel Tyrants here.
Who do most bloudily my life persue;
Who takes my Livelihood, may take that too.
'Gainst little Players you great factions raise,
Make Solemn Leagues and Cov'nants against Plays.
We, who by no Allies assisted are,
Against the Great Confederates must make War.
You need not strive our Province to o'r-run,
By our own Stratagems we are undone.
We've laid out all our Pains, nay Wealth for you,
And yet, hard-hearted men, all will not do.
'Tis not your Judgments sway for you can be
Pleas'd with damn'd Plays (as heart can wish to see)
'Ounds, we do what we can, what won'd you more?
Why do you coxe, and rant, and damn, and roar?
'Sdeath, what a Devil would you have us do?
Each take a Prison, and there humbly sue,
Angling for single Money with a Shoo.
What, will you be Don Johns? have you no remorse?
Farewell then, bloudy men, and take your course.
Yet stay ——
If you'll be civil, we will treat of Peace,
And th' Articles o' th' Treaty shall be these.

"First

" *First, to the men of Wit we all submit;*
The rest shall swagger too within the Pit,
And may roar out their little or no Wit.
But do not 'wear so loud to fright the City,
Who neither care for wicked men, nor witty;
They start at ills they do not like to do,
But shall in Shops be wickeder than you.
" *Next, you'll no more be troubl'd with Machines.*
Item, you shall appear behind our Scenes,
And there make love with the sweet chink of **Guinnies**,
The unresisted Eloquence of Ninnies.
Some of our Women shall be kind to you,
And promise free ingress and egress too.
But if the Faces which we have wo'n't do,
We will find out some of Sixteen for you.
We will be civil when nought else will win ye;
We will new bait our Trap, and that will bring ye.
" *Come, faith let all old breaches now be heal'd,*
And the said Articles shall be Sign'd and Seal'd.

F I N I S.

WS - #0033 - 011021 - C0 - 229/152/6 - PB - 9781334402418